10 THINGS YOU DIDN'T KNOW ABOUT URANUS

A Collection Of Interesting Stories, Facts And Trivia About Mythical Creatures, Unsolved Mysteries, The Human Body, Space And Much More!

Jordan Moore

ISBN: 979-8-88768-018-7

CONTENTS

INTRODUCTION

Welcome to *10 Things You Didn't Know About Uranus*. The book isn't only about *Uranus*, nor is it only about Your Anus. In fact, the book isn't "only about" anything. These pages will cover a variety of delectable delicacies from the world of trivia, sure to set your brain ablaze with extremely (sometimes slightly) interesting information.

However, proceed with caution. You must tackle the subject matter contained within these pages with great maturity and care. You may snicker at the mention of anuses (or is it perhaps ani?). You may even laugh at the world's most revolting cheese. You will certainly giggle uncontrollably at discovering how refusing to emit a foul bottom burp could spell death. But commit your attention to the feast of facts here. They might just save your life, or at least make your friends think you're both intelligent and hilarious.

The point of this book is to tantalize you. The topics are bigger, and more complicated than this book could possibly go into! Your job is to study, examine, and google whatever springs into your imagination while perusing the chapters. You'll discover even more, and you'll be happier (and sillier) for it.

In this book, you are going to learn about literally hundreds of things that are organized into ten convenient chapters. You'll discover real historical mysteries, what makes your gross body work, the world's most revolting foods, and many, many more. Each chapter is set out into ten convenient headings to help you keep track, so don't worry if you lose your place - it's easy enough to find your way again.

Once you have finished attempting to learn about these bizarre topics, remember that you're never done learning! Learning isn't only done within the walls of classrooms, presented by teachers. No! Humans spend their whole lives learning, and it should be a delight to do so.

Hopefully, this is an exciting step toward greater knowledge, or at least it's a step toward having a more enjoyable trip next time you are required upon the porcelain throne.

Please enjoy *10 Things You Didn't Know About Uranus* and remember to keep the book hidden until after you've run around telling everyone about the facts.

THE LONG, SHORT, AND GROSS: THE EXTREMES OF THE HUMAN BODY

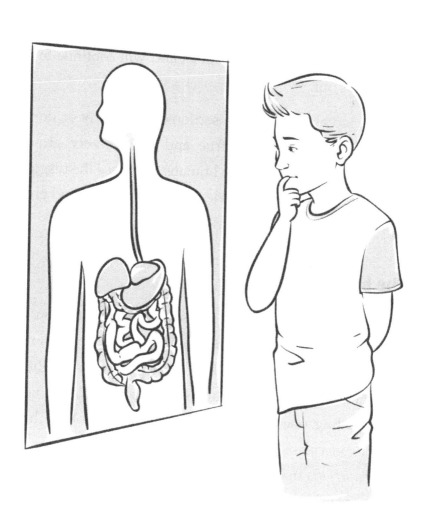

The body you are inhabiting is far from a simple or 'normal' thing. Everyone's body is very different - some are bigger, some smaller; some people have bigger feet and some have a ginormous head. Even if you're not the biggest, tallest, smallest, or ginormousest, your body is far from what one could say is simply 'normal.' In fact, the body that you occupy is an incredible achievement. Congratulations! Your body is, at this moment, performing loads of strange functions and will continue to do so until time runs out.

When you read about these ten sections of strangeness, don't get weirded out. Though it's all true and can be very gross, it's natural and helps us humans be humans. Embrace the disgusting, and enjoy a selection of the weirdest, most incredible, and grossest facts about the human body and its functions.

1. The blinking truth!

On average, a human blinks 20 times a minute. When you blink, you help bring oxygen and hydration to your eye, which means you can see better. Blinking is key to keeping your eye healthy and is something that many animals do. Two muscles, which are the fastest-acting ones in the human body, control the human blink. The *orbicularis oculi* closes your eye while the *levator palpebrae superioris* opens it for you. The whole movement of the blink is over so fast that we don't even notice that we're doing it most of the time. It only takes one-tenth of a second. Over your lifetime, you very well may end up blinking 800,000,000 times!

Given how much work they do, maybe you should thank your eye muscles the next time you perform yet another successful blink.

> **"Thank you, *orbicularis oculi*! Thank you, *levator palpebrae superioris*!"**

Try saying that five times fast.

2. You'll never be the same again

The next fact is a bit strange to think about, so be prepared for that. Perhaps shake your head from side to side a few times and say something random to get in the right state of mind.

Try now to be aware of your whole body. Your eyes reading the page, your hands holding the book, the toes at the ends of your feet. You may even be able to hear your heartbeat or (if you're hungry) your stomach rumbling. Think about every part of the body that is yours and think about how it *is* you. This body is what people see every day, and when they do they think, "Oh! There's ____, I'm glad to see them!"

Here's the freaky thing: this body you're in is *almost* entirely different from the one that you were in a month ago and is *completely different* from the body you were in ten years ago.

Your body (and everything in the world) is made up of trillions upon trillions of microscopic cells. The cells all do different things. You have skin cells, hair cells, cells in your stomach, bone cells, and blood cells, to name just a few. Cells make up everything, even the food you eat, the water you drink, and the air you breathe.

Cells don't last forever, however. Your body performs a lot of functions that cause cells to die off and be replaced by new ones in a process that you'd never, ever notice happening. But this means that you are an animal that is constantly replacing itself with newer versions of itself. You're a regenerating superhero! Within a year, you replace 98% of your own body with newer cells.

- Your skin cells replace themselves every two-four weeks. (**Did You Know?** Household dust is mainly made up of dead human skin cells. Think about that gross fact next time you clean dust off of the table!). The skin is responsible for being the body's first layer of protection, so can come into contact with lots of things that cause it to wear quickly.
- Your liver helps filter things out of liquids and is made of strong and resilient cells, so these replenish every 150–500 days.
- Your stomach cells are constantly doing a lot, and it's difficult to live in your stomach! These unfortunate cells replace themselves every five days or so.
- Your bones are the strange outliers. The bones are constantly regenerating, but it takes a long time and some of your bone cells don't *need* to be replaced for a long time. What is certain, is that every ten years your bone cells have been entirely replaced.

There's more to investigate here! You can find out all sorts about the cells in humans, animals, and plants at school and on the internet. You'd be surprised how much we now know about something that you can't even see.

Isn't it inspiring to know that even if you made a mistake last year - perhaps if you were mean to someone, fell out with your friend, or stole a bar of chocolate - you're 98% different now to that person? So, you can put all those silly mistakes or decisions behind you because you've changed! Almost completely!

3. Measure yourself in the morning...

Speaking of changes, did you know that at 9 a.m. you are very different from how you are at 4 p.m.? You may be thinking, "Well, yes, I know that. Me at 9 a.m. is tired and me at 4 p.m. is hungry." There are other differences, though.

On average, you are just under half an inch taller when you wake up than at the end of the day. This is due to something called cartilage. Cartilage is a soft material between your bones. It helps protect your bones and joints by acting as an absorber and barrier between your bones. It essentially helps you to walk, hold things, point, and draw! When you've woken up, your cartilage has relaxed overnight, stretched, and is thicker. But after a day of walking around, your cartilage compresses and becomes smaller as you work your body. This means you lose just under half an inch of padding between your bones across your body, so you're that much smaller by the time you go back to bed!

4. ...And buy your shoes in the afternoon

A rule for life that you should forever abide by from now on is to only buy new shoes in the afternoon, never in the morning. The reason for this is very simple. As you go about your day, blood moves around your body, which helps to keep you active. As you walk around and move throughout your day, the blood rushes to your feet and makes them grow or *engorge*. Some people's feet can engorge so much that they gain half a shoe size! So, if you want comfortable shoes, make sure you buy them in the afternoon and not in the morning.

5. Moaning about hormones!

If you want to understand why you act the way you act and feel the way you feel, then you must learn about hormones and what they do in your body throughout the day. They are incredible! Hormones are substances that are created by your body and released to help you perform different tasks. Your body is constantly producing them depending on what you need to do, and they guide your day more than you could know.

The hormone *cortisol* helps you digest food in order to release energy for you. Your body releases lots of cortisol at the start of the day, to give you an enormous boost in the morning so you can start your day well. But it's not being used much in the evening. So, if you weigh yourself in the morning and the evening, you'll notice that 'evening' you is far heavier than 'morning' you!

Serotonin is another incredible hormone. It has a massive impact on your day; unbelievably, it dictates whether you're going to be happy or not. Serotonin helps decide our mood, alertness, body function, and many other things too. Scientists have worked out that we release lots of serotonin at about midday, so you'll be at your most alert (and your happiest) then. If you can, you should try to do tasks and work during the middle of the day to be the most productive! Serotonin wears off later in the day and *melatonin* kicks in. This tells you it's time for bed, and your body will begin preparation for deep sleep.

6. Haven't I read this before?

Have you ever experienced déjà vu before? You may have done so but just weren't aware of its name.

Did you ever see or live through something that you were sure you'd done before? Not similarly, but *exactly the same*? Well, this is called déjà vu. Déjà vu is a French term that means "already seen."

It's difficult to know why déjà vu happens. Some people maintain that we're all a bit psychic and we sometimes get a quick look into the future, but scientists aren't convinced.

The answer that seems the most likely is that our brain makes a mistake in its memory-management. Think of the brain as having two boxes that it puts memories into. It has short-term memory and long-term memory. Everything goes into the short-term box first before it is put into the long-term box. We use our memories in the long-term box to help us in our lives. The theory is that déjà vu happens when our brains accidentally put the memory directly into the long-term box, which means we *think* that we've already done it before when we haven't. This leads to us having a moment of certainty where we swear that we've experienced precisely the same situation before, even though we haven't.

No one is 100% certain, though. Déjà vu remains a bit of a mystery! Perhaps we are psychic after all?

7. Falling off a cliff, or falling off your bed?

Sleeping is a natural part of our daily life and ensuring you get the proper amount of sleep is really important for just about everything! But there are areas of our sleep that remain a bit of a conundrum.

For instance, you may have had the feeling before of feeling wonderfully tired and drifting off to sleep. The light has been blocked out, your tasks for the day are complete, and the pillow embraces you as you head toward the land of nod. All is calm, all is well. Then...

WHOA!

You suddenly jolt awake, pulled away from sleep and in a mild panic, wondering what on earth happened.

This is called the *"hypnic jerk"* or *"sleep start,"* and it is estimated that seven out of ten people experience them. The sleep start can often feel like you're falling and can be a very abrupt interruption to your sleep.

There's nothing wrong if you experience this – it's quite normal - the only question is why does it happen? The answer is that we're not too sure. The guess is that your brain misunderstands your relaxing and thinks something is wrong. So, it jolts you awake, trying to rapidly bring you to a state of alert. This may be the correct answer, but it's all guesswork. Perhaps you have a theory?

8. Remembering dreams is like holding smoke

While on the subject of sleep, have you ever tried to think about your dreams once you've woken up? Perhaps to see if you can work out what they mean, or to just remind yourself that though it was scary, it's all over now and isn't real?

This is very normal. Dreams occur for all humans, at every age, and in many animals as well. We know a lot about dreams, but there are many aspects that remain unknown. Here are a few key facts about dreaming and dreams that may help you work out what it's all about:

- Dreams are based on your memories. Every human face you see in a dream is the face of someone you've actually seen before!
- You dream in the morning, just before you wake up, in the REM (Rapid Eye Movement) stage of your sleep. You

11

remember these dreams well once you wake up, partly because they've only just happened to you.

- You'll have nicer dreams if you're happier. If you're a bit stressed out or having a bad few days, that's likely to show up in your dreams too.

- It's more common to have a negative dream than a positive one. There are a few reasons this could be, but it's likely that the fear center of your brain is heavily engaged in dreaming.

- You can take control of your dreams. The process is known as *lucid dreaming*, and it's possible to learn how to do it! Those who can do it easily can use their time dreaming to work through problems and create elaborate stories in their dreams.

- You'll forget most of your dreams. Dreams that repeat will be easier to remember, but many dreams simply disappear from our memories.

Dreams can feel a bit scary or confusing at times. But it's important to remember that they're more likely to be random than to be anything helpful. So, don't spend too long wondering what it all means!

9. Gradually turning into Dumbo

Have you ever noticed that old men and women can have very large ears and noses? Next time you see an elderly person, stop and look (but do so in a kind manner - don't stop and point at them).

This isn't unusual. In fact, you'll end up that way yourself one day!

Your height will eventually stop growing once you reach your mid to late teenage years, and you're likely to remain at that height for the rest of your life. But your nose and ears continue to grow throughout your life!

The reason for this is that gravity continues to act on these parts of your body. Gravity is a force that drags everything back toward the center of the earth. It's why you're not flying toward the moon at the moment! Gravity causes your nose and ears to sag over time, so after 70, 80, or 90 years, the features are longer and droopier.

10. Never look inside yourself, it's gross

Humans' insides are pretty disgusting. Ideally, you will never have to look at all the bits that go on under the surface because honestly, it's gross.

But it's also exceptionally interesting and kind of unbelievable. The human is an almost-perfect organism, able to adapt to different environments, survive a range of situations, and bend the world to its will. But how? Here are a few bizarre facts about the goings-on within your very body:

- You're born with more bones when you're a baby than you have when you're an adult. Babies are born with about 300 bones in their body, and some of the bones fuse together as they grow, which leaves you with 206 when you're an adult.

- All of your organs either come in pairs (kidneys, lungs, eyes) or a singular count (heart, brain, liver); a human could lose one of their paired organs (one kidney, one lung, one eye), and they would continue to be able to live (though you could lose both your eyes and live as well!).

- If you were to unravel your small intestine (don't do it) it would be about 23 feet long, half the length of the Hollywood sign!

- Your blood vessels are tube-like structures that help carry blood throughout your body, passing through the organs and keeping you alive. You need quite a lot of these to keep you going. In fact, you need so many that if you were to lay all the vessels you find in an adult on the ground from end-to-end, it would stretch to 100,000 miles in length.

- On average, a person produces a liter of spit every day. Yuck! This means that, throughout your life, you could fill two swimming pools with your saliva. Don't try to do this, however, or you'll never be allowed back in by the lifeguard.

That was just a short look into some of the disgusting, interesting, and bizarre facts about the human body. You could write books and books on the matter, and we'd still never get bored of it! You'll find out even more about it as you research, but why not gross your friends out by bringing up one of the facts you learned here the next time you see them? They won't thank you, but you'll look very clever.

A SELECTION OF THE GREATEST UNSOLVED MYSTERIES EVER

Have you ever watched *Scooby Doo* before? The show is about a team of mystery investigators and their dog. They zoom around, in their minivan, solving mysteries across the world, saving people from confusing and frightening experiences. Scooby and the gang always win - they always find out who's been pretending to be a ghoul or who is the axe-wielding murderer. Scooby Doo is amazing!

However, in human history, sometimes the answer is never revealed. There have been many occasions where the gang could have helped solve a real-life mystery. In this chapter, you'll hear true stories about murders, prison escapes, and monsters. In each case, there is no answer to be found, and people are continuing to investigate them to this very day.

Here are several true, still unsolved mysteries that have occupied the minds of scientists, historians, and casual readers for tens and, sometimes, hundreds of years. Please enjoy reading about some spooky, baffling, and downright riveting true mysteries.

1. Jack the Ripper

Jack the Ripper is very probably the most famous mystery of all time and for good reason. The case in its fullest is unpleasant, and who 'Jack' actually was is a mystery that's never been solved.

Cast your minds to 1888, London, UK. Over the last 100 years, London has changed a great deal. The air was thick with black smoke, crime had risen year after year, and the wealthy were becoming wealthier by the hour with little care for others. For the poor in London, life was hard, filled with the threat of sickness and low wages. Robberies were common in the twisting pathways that formed the maze-like city, and worse still, murder was a very real possibility.

The Metropolitan Police Force, who were only a recent creation, faced their greatest challenge yet when, on August 31, 1888, stories circulated in London of a horrific murder.

Citizens had found a woman in the early hours of the morning, the victim of an attack, and the papers immediately printed accounts of a 'Monster' in the area of Whitechapel. People whispered to each other about the grisly matter, and the story of the murder became a popular conversation on street corners, in public houses, and on building sites. Matters worsened when, on September 8, 1888, another body was discovered.

The victim was once again female and the whole affair seemed similar to the incident from only a week earlier. The difference this time was that a man had been spotted, only moments before the murder, talking to her. He wore a long coat and a hat, but details of his face weren't recorded by the eyewitness. The people of London were obsessed with the case, the police force had no luck so far, and families began to impose curfews on the young women in their households.

For the next three weeks, things quietened down and some of the panic in East London abated. Perhaps it was all over now? Unfortunately, not.

On September 30, 1888, two separate women were discovered dead and declared victims of the same killer. Unrest increased in the East End, and detectives worked around the clock, desperately searching for the elusive culprit. The papers loved the drama caused by the whole affair, making money across the country with their reports from London. Only a week later, a fifth woman was discovered on November 9, 1888.

This marked the end of the work of Jack. Perhaps he was imprisoned for a different crime, he passed away himself, or he left the country. Whatever happened, no one was ever arrested for the series of crimes and the crimes became a legendary story of Victorian London.

To this day, historians obsess over the case, desperately hoping that if they work hard enough, they may discover who the man was. Every so often, a book is released with 'the true identity.' But there will likely never be a discovery of who did it. The police in 1888 weren't equipped with the technology we have nowadays and didn't keep pieces of evidence that could have been extremely helpful to the case in the future.

There are theories he was a doctor, that he had come from another country in Europe, or was a policeman. But the mystery of Jack the Ripper remains, with the image of a silhouetted man in a long coat shrouded in smoke, stalking the streets of London, living on in Londoners' minds.

2. The disappearance of D. B. Cooper

The next mystery takes place in a more modern time, 1971 to be precise. It doesn't involve grisly murders, or speculative Londoners, no. In fact, this mystery unfolded 10,000 feet in the air, surrounded by witnesses, and has baffled the FBI for over 50 years.

On November 24, 1971, Flight 305 departed from Portland, Oregon destined for Seattle, Washington. It was a slightly miserable day, being quite rainy and cold, but this was expected for November. There were six crew members and 37 passengers onboard the plane and as the aircraft soared into the sky, a man sat in 18-E ordered a drink.

The man was dressed in a dark suit, with a white shirt and black tie. He had a raincoat with him and was carrying a briefcase. He was slim, in his 40s, white, and seemed relatively normal. He'd bought a ticket for this particular flight earlier that day using cash, and the name on the ticket was Dan Cooper. He leaned over to an air stewardess called Florence Schaffner and handed her a note.

Florence had experience of businessmen handing her their phone number, hoping that she might accompany them for a drink after the journey, so pocketed the note without looking. Before she could walk away, to commence with another task, Cooper leaned over to her and said, "Miss you'd better look at that note. I have a bomb."

Carefully, Florence looked at the note. It asked her to sit next to him and also contained those same words Cooper had just spoken to her:

I have a bomb.

Florence sat down and Cooper showed her the inside of his briefcase. It had tubes of what looked like dynamite in it and many wires. Cooper told Florence that he didn't want to detonate the bomb at all and asked her to tell the captain what he wanted. Florence wrote down the demands. He'd requested:

- $200,000 in cash
- Two parachutes
- For the plane to land in Seattle, refuel and then proceed on course to Mexico City, using his plan.

Florence took the demands to the captain, who contacted Air Traffic Control and relayed the demands. In the meantime, a flight attendant called Tina Mucklow sat next to Cooper.

On the flight to the airport, as the FBI was gathering together the demands, Mucklow spoke with Cooper. She said he was very relaxed, talking about the scenery, and didn't seem agitated. Strange for a man who had just hijacked a plane and was looking at a life sentence in prison if he was caught!

Upon arrival in Seattle, the plane was refueled, and the passengers were released from the plane. The man asked for Mucklow to stay on the plane, along with the pilots, but released all other members of the crew. Mucklow collected the parachutes and money, bringing them back to Cooper. Cooper offered Mucklow some money, but she refused, stating it was against company policy to accept a cash tip.

The flight set off once more and began to head south. Jets were deployed, who followed the plane out of Cooper's vision. At 7 p.m., Cooper told Mucklow to go to the cabin with the pilots and not return. He promised that she'd be safe; he'd either deactivate the bomb or it'd come with him. Mucklow did so and shortly after, a warning light came on in the cabin. A back door was open!

The pilot used the intercom to ask Cooper if he needed help, and a curt response came from the hijacker:

"No."

That was the last anyone ever saw or heard of D. B. Cooper. To this day, no one knows what happened to him after he left the aircraft. Did he survive the fall? Did he start a new life somewhere in America? Was Cooper even his name? All these questions were asked and investigated, but no one knew what truly happened to him. The FBI spent 45 years looking for this criminal but to no avail.

D. B. Cooper's disappearance remains the only unsolved case of air piracy. He lives on as a bit of a criminal legend for his seemingly charming manner and lack of aggression. You can make your own ending up to his story and you'll be just as correct as anyone. What do you think happened after he jumped?

3. The man on Somerton Beach

This story sounds like a made-up detective story and remains a little bit spooky. So, get ready for spooky town, and read the case of the Man from Somerton Beach.

Adelaide in Australia was known as the '20-minute city' because everything is 20 minutes from the city center. Supposedly, in a mere 20 minutes, you can access housing, shopping, hikes, and the beach. It was on Somerton Beach that, in December 1948, a body was discovered slumped against a wall. The man was dressed in a lovely, clean suit and had polished, smart shoes on. If it wasn't for the fact he wasn't moving, he'd have seemed perfectly normal.

The authorities examined the body to find the identity but were stumped. He had no identification documents, no wallet, no money, no tickets, no passport - there weren't even any tags on his clothing! The police released a photograph of the man's face, pleading for answers, but no answers came in from anyone. They couldn't even work out how he'd died. Perhaps a heart attack? There were no wounds and no poison in his system.

The detectives were baffled; there were so many questions and so few answers to be found. That is until they found a hidden pocket sewn into the inside of the man's trousers four months later. The small pocket had a piece of paper in it that had two printed words on it:

Tamám Shud

The words mean 'it has ended' and were taken from a rare book of translated Persian poems. The piece of paper had been taken from a book; it wasn't hand-written, but printed. The police searched for the *exact* copy of the book but found nothing until eight months later.

A local man walked into the police station holding a copy of the rare book. He said that the book had turned up in his car, which he had parked near Somerton Beach, just after they had discovered the body. He'd thought little about it until the papers had printed that a strange note had been found on the body, and he remembered the strange book. Sure enough, there were two words cut out of it. There was a gap where there should have been "Tamám Shud."

The book also contained a cryptic code and a phone number. The number led to a woman called Jessica Thompson, who admitted to selling a copy of the book to a man called Alfred Boxall. But Boxall was still alive and still had that copy, so the phone number ended up being no help at all. The cryptic code was never solved, rendering it useless to the investigation.

The case is still unsolved, though there was a development in 2022. Professor Derek Abbott of Adelaide University claims to have identified the unknown man as an engineer by the name of Carl "Charles" Webb, using the man's DNA.

Even if his name is indeed Carl Webb, there are still so many questions about the case. The mysterious code, note, phone number, book, and cause of death are all unsolved. Perhaps with confirmation of identity, more information will unfold as time goes by, but given that it's almost been 80 years since the case opened, perhaps not.

4. The mysterious ghost ship Mary Celeste

What could be scarier than an old ship full of scurvy pirates? How about an old ship with no one on it? The following story is about the mysterious fate of *Mary Celeste* and its crew, a case that has no confirmed answer but plenty of theories about ghosts, monsters, and earthquakes.

The *Mary Celeste* was a ship that helped transport goods across the ocean and was constantly in use after it was launched in 1861. It was set for a routine voyage on November 5, 1872, as Captain Briggs, his wife, child, and a crew of seven sailors prepared to sail from New York, America to Genoa, Italy.

The ship was carrying 1,700 barrels of alcohol, an expensive cargo. The captain and his wife were excited to experience the long journey and he had promised to write to his mother to tell her of the amazing things that would surely happen along the way.

It so happened another boat departed on a similar journey as the *Mary Celeste* only eight days later. The ship was called *Dei Gratia* and was following the same route, manned by Captain Morehouse. On December 4, 1872, Morehouse came to the deck of his boat to find a concerned helmsman. The sailor told him that they had spotted a vessel slowly drifting toward the *Dei Gratia*.

Morehouse recognized the ship as the *Mary Celeste*; he was aware of Captain Briggs and was concerned. The ships drew closer, and there was no one on deck, as far as Morehouse could tell. Captain Morehouse sent sailors to the *Mary Celeste* on a small boat and asked them to investigate. Their reports returned more questions than answers.

The ship was deserted. No living or dead sailor was on board. The single lifeboat, big enough for the whole crew, was missing and the sails were in poor condition. There was a small amount of water sloshing around inside, but that was quite normal; other than a few knocks and broken objects, the ship was okay.

The captain's log remained on the ship. Logs were used by the captain to record how the journey was going, chart their progress, and write down anything important. The last recorded log was on November 25, nine days earlier, which gave the ship's coordinates but nothing else. Captain Briggs' personal items were still there, but his navigational equipment had disappeared along with the ship's legal documents.

The cargo of alcohol remained, the equipment had been put away neatly, and there were at least six months of provisions on board still. It seemed as though the crew had, quite calmly, proceeded to the lifeboat and disappeared. Morehouse decided to bring the boat to Gibraltar with him and after a long, painful journey, the two vessels arrived on December 12.

There was an investigation, and numerous theories were thrown around about what could have happened:

- The first thought was that the crew had turned on Captain Briggs, but if that was the case, why would they leave the ship?
- Piracy was suspected, then dismissed. Why was there no sign of aggression or violence on board? Also, the cargo was still there; pirates would certainly have taken it.

After these possibilities were removed, the agreement was that something extraordinary and alarming must have happened for the crew to leave the ship. But what? This is where the theories range from sensible to a bit crazy:

- Perhaps there was a small explosion from one of the alcohol barrels. Then everyone evacuated onto the boat, which drifted away into the open ocean.
- Maybe a sudden iceberg emerged, and the ship was abandoned, though not struck.
- A small earthquake under the ocean could have startled the sailors.
- A giant squid attacked the ship.
- All the people killed themselves for an unknown reason.
- One person survived, but the rest were eaten by sharks.

No one knows the fate of the occupants of the *Mary Celeste*, and there have been so many made-up accounts from people who claim to be on the crew that such information is difficult to believe. Arthur Conan Doyle (author of *Sherlock Holmes*) even wrote a book about it…, that was almost entirely lies!

You can decide for yourself what the most likely reason was! (Though it probably wasn't a giant squid.)

5. Escape from Alcatraz

If you've ever read or seen the *Harry Potter* series, then you might be aware of the magical prison *Azkaban*. The inescapable prison is for evil wizards and is located on a small island, surrounded by harsh waters, and guarded by brutal guards. Well, this is actually based on a famous, real-life prison called Alcatraz, and is the home to one of the most captivating escape attempts ever.

The island of Alcatraz used to be a military base until it was turned into a prison in 1934. It is located about a mile and a half from the coast of San Francisco. The water around Alcatraz is bone-chillingly cold, which meant that escape was assumed impossible. After all, how would anyone be able to survive a mile and a half swimming in ice-cold water?

In 1962, three men thought they'd give it a shot anyway.

Their names were Frank Morris, John Anglin, and Clarence Anglin. They'd all earned their sentence in Alcatraz for robberies. Frank had a difficult childhood, but the Anglin family earned a good deal of money from farming and the brothers developed a reputation as exceptional swimmers. They would amaze their other siblings by swimming in frozen lakes.

The elaborate escape plan is an incredible story and took over two years for the prisoners to pull off. They needed to make sure that three different elements were in place before they could try it:

1) Three fake heads, which would fool the guards into thinking they were still in their beds. They created them from a mix of materials including concrete, papier mâché, and soap. Clarence worked as a barber, so was able to procure some hair for the dummy heads.

2) A way out of their cells. Each cell had a small vent on the back wall. The vent was small, but they spent months drilling and chipping away at the holes to make them wide enough to fit out of.

3) A way off of the island. There was no way that any of them could survive the swim; not the whole way, anyway. So, they spent a year gathering raincoats, with which the prisoners were provided. They managed to procure about 50 of them and sewed them together to form a raft that could float.

They had a diversion, they had a way out of the prison, and they had a way off of the island. They were ready.

The date was June 11, 1962. The morning bell rang through the prison for the inmates to rise from their beds for breakfast, but three cells in Cell Block B remained undisturbed as the prisoners shuffled toward the canteen. The guards laughed with each other about the lazy, sleepy prisoners and left them alone in their beds. If they didn't want breakfast, so be it!

After a few hours, the guards had had enough and one reached into the cell of Frank Morris and pushed his head, telling him to get up. The guard stood with his mouth agape, like a monkey staring at his own reflection, as Frank's head rolled off of the bed and onto the floor. The guard gathered himself for a second and realized the head was fake. The alarm was instantly sounded, and the guards rushed into the remaining two cells of the Anglin brothers. Empty!

As a thorough sweep of the prison was conducted, the FBI arrived at Alcatraz. They found the widened air ducts, which led into a service tunnel, where they found the men's tools. The investigators then located an open vent in the ceiling of the tunnel, through which the men had clambered onto the roof. From the roof, they'd jumped the fence and set off.

No one has located the raft and the prisoners to this day. Frank, John, and Clarence are all still on the FBI Most Wanted list. The FBI receives calls from time to time from people claiming to have information. All the calls and investigating have led to nothing.

The big question after reading about the great escape has to be: What happened after they escaped? There are three major possibilities, each of which has been considered by the authorities:

- The raft didn't work, and the three men died in their escape attempt. The FBI says this is the most likely, though no bodies nor 50 raincoats have ever been found.
- They reached San Francisco and started new lives under new names in America. Perhaps they stole a car and forged phony documents. Despite several apparent 'sightings,' none of these have ever been confirmed. So, if this is true, they've done it very well.
- They managed to find a way into another country, to start again there. They would have found it difficult to board a plane in the state they must have been in after their escape, but it's possible.

No one knows, of course. But the escape was extremely famous. In 1963, the author J. Campbell Bruce wrote a book documenting the escape called *Escape from Alcatraz* and a film by the same name was later produced. You're welcome to consider any ending for the story that you like. the case is officially closed with no answer.

Don't tell any young friends about it though. They might get ideas for the next time they want to sneak out to visit a friend at night.

6. The Bermuda Triangle

The following tale continues to frighten some people into refusing to get onto planes to this day. Countless documentaries have been created about it. This is a story about the Bermuda Triangle.

In the North Atlantic Ocean, there is a triangular area between Miami, Bermuda, and Puerto Rico that has been the site of great mystery over the last century. It is reported that inside the triangle, a number of ships and aircraft have completely disappeared without explanation. Countless theories have emerged as to why vehicles struggle in this area, from sea monsters to strong magnetic fields.

The most famous case of disappearance comes from 1945 when Flight 19 vanished. Flight 19 was the collective name for five U.S. Navy Bombers who were lost during a training mission. A further rescue aircraft was sent out into the triangle to find them, but that team vanished as well. Stories such as this have led the triangle to develop a fearful, supernatural reputation among mystery enthusiasts the world over.

Speculation over the causes of the disappearance includes several logical answers. For instance, the triangle may be home to sudden weather changes that knock planes off course, or magnetic fields make the compasses and navigational equipment fail. There are also several less likely answers, such as it being the home to a society of aliens who shoot the planes, or some demonic or ghostly entity.

Either way, the Bermuda Triangle remains an eerie spot on the map and one that many pilots and passengers will not fly over, ever. Would you feel confident enough to get on a plane that you know is going through it?

7. Loch Ness Monster

If you visit Scotland, particularly a small and isolated area near Inverness, then you'll hear rumblings of a fearsome creature that eludes even the smartest scientists and is directly descended from the dinosaurs. The frightening, prehistoric creature is called Nessie!

The story of the Loch Ness Monster (or more affectionately, Nessie) is a legendary tale that has managed to stand the test of time through the last century. Several eyewitnesses claim that, within Loch Ness (a lake), there is an animal that inhabits the waters. The creature looks a bit like a cross between a serpent and a dinosaur, with a long, protruding neck and large humps all along its back. It feasts on whatever it can find within its waters, which are fed by the River Ness.

There is a famous photograph of Nessie, which looks a bit like the description written here. But the photo is 99% likely to be a complete fake. Explorers and navigators have charted the waters of Loch Ness, using advanced scientific equipment to study the likelihood of the monster existing. Fish numbers have been recorded, the riverbank surveyed, and radar has been employed to try to catch sight of the elusive animal. But nothing conclusive has been found.

Some in Scotland believe that Nessie is a surviving dinosaur, somehow left behind during the great extinction event. Others believe that it's not a monster at all, but instead a large eel or an animal that has been identified incorrectly.

If you tell the people of Inverness about the 'logical' answers and refuse to believe it's a dinosaur, you'll be quickly dismissed for your failure to believe. Old-timers will swear on The Bible that the creature possesses magical powers that mean it can disappear, or it has access to an intricate tunnel system underneath the Loch that allows it to elude the scientists.

Thousands flock to see Nessie every year - or try to, at least. People love to listen to eyewitness accounts from the early 1900s or hear a tour guide swear that they've seen unexplainable phenomena within the waters. Nessie is an enduring and important part of Scottish folklore. She'll be around for decades to come, whether she's real or not.

8. The Roswell UFO incident

Have you ever wondered where the stereotypical image of aliens, with long, slender bodies, jet-black eyes, and green or grey skin comes from? Well, it came into popular use in the 1950s in the wake of an event known as the Roswell Incident, which occurred in 1947.

In Roswell, New Mexico, a local farmer known as Mack Brazel was out surveying his ranch when he saw a series of bizarre things that he'd never seen before. It looked like debris; pieces of metal and materials that had ended up on his property somehow. The material was shiny and made of something that he couldn't fully explain. He ran to the local sheriff's office to report what had happened to the police and to ask for help.

The Army Airfield was notified, and they all met on Brazel's ranch to examine the wreckage. The military released a statement saying that they'd found 'A Flying Disc' on the ranch, and rumors shot with surprising speed through the population of Roswell. An Unidentified Flying Object had been found! A sighting of alien aircraft, admitted by the military and the police - incredible!

However, the military changed their story shortly afterwards and refuted that there was anything alien happening on the ranch. Instead, they said that a weather balloon had crashed and bits of debris had fallen into the ranch. It was a false alarm, they said, and nothing to worry about. Too little, too late.

The rumors were already out there. Millions of people by now had heard of the story, as well as the latest 'excuse' from the military, and they weren't buying it. There were calls for the truth to be unveiled - it must be a cover-up!

Before too long, stories began to emerge from Roswell locals. Grown men swore on their mothers' lives to have seen strange, pulsating lights in the sky while others promised they'd actually seen aliens walking around Roswell! Investigators and historians have examined the crash site countless times, listened to every testimony, and considered all of the evidence. But there's no conclusive answer.

Some maintain that it was indeed a weather balloon and that a crash isn't uncommon. Others say that the evidence of that is weak, pointing to the attempted cover-up from the military. Either way, every year Roswell is visited by thousands who want to see where aliens did (or did not) visit Earth. There's even an annual alien festival!

Whether it's true or not, this story reminds us of the vastness of the universe and our place within it. We are curious about the endlessness of it all, the unending reach of space, and the countless planets across billions and billions of miles of nothingness.

Surely it can't just be us here, right?

9. The biggest henge of them all

If you drive through England, along one of the major highways there, you'll spot one of the world's biggest and most famous henges. What is a henge? That doesn't matter, but Stonehenge does matter. (*For your interest – it's a circular area, often containing a circle of stones or sometimes wooden posts, dating from the Neolithic and Bronze Ages.*)

Stonehenge is a collection of colossal rectangular blocks, carved out of stone, that are organized into a large circle. The stone has likely been in position for almost 2,000 years.

Here's the mystery: No one is sure who put them there. Each stone is colossal and weighs 25 tons on average, which is about the weight of 16 mid-sized cars. It's certain that the whole thing was constructed for some sort of religious or spiritual purpose, but who and how? How do you lift such a heavy weight without any machinery or automation?

Even stranger than that is where the stone came from. We know that the stone was likely from South Wales, which means it was transported about 120 miles.

So, what we know about Stonehenge is that a lot of exceptionally heavy stone was taken over 120 miles away from where it was from and arranged in a massive circle for a purpose that we can't work out.

There are many theories as to Stonehenge's origins. Historians estimate that the structure was built by Pagans, an old religious group that largely doesn't exist anymore. They prayed to many gods and were driven out of England by the Christians a long time ago. Other, more zany predictions state that it was aliens! Whoever it was must have been incredibly clever to have figured out a way to transport so much stone, so far. (For your interest: *Stonehenge was built by descendants of Neolithic migrants, DNA study shows.*)

People continue to visit Stonehenge to this day, to marvel at the structure, and to celebrate vaguely pagan festivals throughout the year. It's common to see the celebrations of the Winter and Summer solstice there, the shortest and longest days of the year.

One thing is for sure, Stonehenge is an incredibly impressive part of history, no matter who got it there or how they did it.

10. The Voynich Manuscript

There's nothing better to a group of historians than a good book. Even better if that book is mysterious and vaguely spooky.

In the early 20th century, a man called Wilfrid Voynich discovered a book, which he went on to name after himself. Voynich was a book dealer and often found himself in possession of rare works of literature, which he then sold for an *enormous* profit. But there was something off about this particular piece.

The book is written in a language that neither Voynich nor anyone else for that matter has been able to work out. Likely, it's written in code, rather than a formal language. The book is covered in bizarre illustrations of strange plants, star charts, and unexplained diagrams.

After decades of research, we now know that it comes from the 15th century after the book was carbon-dated. The assumption is that it's Italian, but everything else is unknown and up for debate. One theory says that it was written by some sort of alchemist or a person who wanted to work with black magic or summon the devil. Another theory is that some Italian guy was having a good laugh, made a strange book, and that was that.

The book is now housed at Yale University and has undergone a drastic amount of study. It's preserved carefully and studied by cartographers from across the world. To discover what the book is about would be incredible. It may possess great knowledge of the past or secrets of some organization hitherto not understood. It could possess nothing of any worth at all, of course; maybe just a recipe for delicious bread.

But it's a testament to the curiosity that all humans have. We love mystery and intrigue, and we particularly like it when there's no answer yet. What do you think the strange manuscript says? What mysterious words are etched into those pages?

That's the end of the mysteries!

In the wilderness of time and history, there is far more to discover than what we had time for here. If any of these tales tickled your fancy in particular, then researching them could be great fun - but do make sure you check with whoever is in charge of your household first. Some of the mysteries mentioned above can be very difficult to read about or are sincerely unpleasant. Plus, learning is always the most fun when we do it together.

As you google, read, and go 'huh,' find other mysteries as you go along. But as you do so, think critically. What's the most likely answer? Is the answer *really* going to be aliens? Or is there likely a far simpler explanation? Either way, hopefully, you have enjoyed having the detective side of your brain tantalized in this chapter of mystery and confusion.

WHAT ARE YOU SCARED OF?

Are you scared of anything? You may confidently tell your pals that you're 'not scared of anything!' But chances are that's not true.

In this chapter, you will read a lot of extremely interesting facts about fear. You'll learn why we experience fear, what happens when we come across something scary, and how fear can develop into a serious condition for some people. It's important to remember to be sensitive to what you read in this chapter and learn what you can about an instinct that we all have as human beings.

1. What happens when animals are scared?

Almost all humans have a fear of something. Fear is perfectly normal and can lead us to make better decisions, but where does it come from? Why are we scared of things?

Many animals have an instinct within them that activates when they're scared. It's called fight or flight. It's normally a quick decision that's made under stress and the decision is whether to *fight* the thing or *run away* from it. Most animals have the instinct and humans are no different.

Think of something that might make you scared and how you may react to it. If you're scared of the dark, then you would decide that you can't fight it, so you must run away from it to safety. If you're scared of a spider, then you may instead decide to get rid of the spider using a cup and a piece of card. The spider isn't much of a threat, you just don't like it, so you remove it and *fight* the phobia.

2. Why do we become frightened?

This decision all happens within the brain, in a place called the amygdala. The amygdala triggers your nervous system, and hormones (we talked about these in chapter one!) get released that make you alert. Your heart beats faster, you breathe faster, and your blood starts to pump quickly to your limbs. You prepare to either run or fight.

The amygdala can be set off by all manner of different things, and it's very dependent on who you are. While there are common things that scare many people, such as the dark or heights, everyone is fearful of other things that are rarely shared.

3. What is a phobia?

Many humans suffer from things called phobias, and there are literally thousands of them. A phobia is a particular, specific thing that scares people, and it can develop for many different reasons.

Phobias differ from simply 'being scared.' People who have phobias may act in strange ways to avoid what they have a phobia of, such as refusing to be involved with situations such as flying, funerals, or parties. The word originates from the Greek word *phobos*, which means 'fear' or 'horror,' and it helps accurately describe people who have experienced phobias. Read on further to find out what happens to people with phobias, and how we can all help.

4. Common phobias

Here are some examples of the most common phobias, and a small explanation as to why they may happen:

- Acrophobia – an intense fear of heights, the most common phobia in the world. Many people are scared of heights, but people with acrophobia will avoid heights altogether if possible.

- Arachnophobia – the fear of spiders. Many people are scared of spiders, perhaps because our ancestors would have had good reason to be. People thousands of years ago could get bitten by a venomous spider and get very sick or die, so it was best to avoid them.

- Cynophobia – a fear of dogs. For some people (usually dog owners), it may seem odd to be scared of a little fluffy woof machine, but this can be a difficult phobia to live with. It usually comes from an experience as a child, perhaps being bitten by a dog, which leaves the person very scared of dogs, no matter how fluffy or cute.

- Claustrophobia – a fear of small spaces. This common phobia is the fear of being trapped in a space, usually one that's too small to be comfortable in. We could all understand being scared of being trapped in a *very* small space like a cupboard or coffin. But this can also make people scared of being stuck inside a bedroom or house. This often comes from childhood if they had an experience of feeling trapped.

- Necrophobia – a fear of death-related things. It's very common for people to fear death because we don't know what happens after it. People with this fear will also be scared of graveyards, dead animals, and even funerals. There are many reasons this may occur such as an unpleasant experience with death or even depictions in movies.

- Trypanophobia – a fear of needles. It's not too difficult to work out why people are scared of needles. When we're very young, most of us will have injections to stop us from becoming very sick in the future, and the process is painful. We don't like pain, and because we don't get injections often, we usually remember it being worse than it really is.

5. Why your childhood can make you scared?

If you're paying attention, you'll have noticed that most causes of phobias come from experiences in our lives. If you have an unpleasant experience with something, then it's possible to become frightened of it and have bad reactions to it. However, there are other reasons that we develop phobias.

Did you know that your family has a massive part to play in dictating what scares you? When you're little, you learn about how to act by copying adults and other children; so, if your parents react by screaming when they see a spider, what are you going to do? It might be worth talking to your family about what they're scared of, or whether they have any phobias. You may find that you've picked up something from them!

6. Who you are can make you scared

As well as this, scientists now think that your genetics can play a major role in deciding what you're scared of. Your genetics is a word for the 'stuff' that makes you, into you! Your parents, and their parents, and their parents, and so on and so forth, passed your genetics down over time. As a result, you are composed of dozens of people who stretch back through time. We all have certain things about us that have been passed down over hundreds of years, which could include how sensitive you are towards scary things. So, if you're scared of something that others think is harmless, you can blame your great-great-great-grandmother!

7. Society can increase your fears too!

Where you live also may play a part in your fears. The country you live in is unique! It has its own rules and behaviors, which can influence who you are. If it's difficult to access a hospital or doctor in your country, then you'll probably be more scared of becoming ill. If you're from an area where there's not much money to be earned, then you may become scared of inequality or struggling with finances. If your country has suffered from war, then you may develop a fear of violence and anger.

These all play a part in deciding what you're scared of and can easily lead to someone developing a phobia of something.

8. Some less-than-common phobias

We must treat phobias sensitively. The fear is very real for people with phobias, and there are several very strange-sounding phobias that do affect people's lives. Here's a short list of less common ones compared to the above. Can you think why someone may be scared of some of these?

- Arachibutyrophobia – the fear of peanut butter sticking to the roof of your mouth
- Ombrophobia – the fear of rain
- Spectrophobia – the fear of mirrors and reflections
- Nomophobia – the fear of being without a cell phone
- Hippopotomonstrosesquippedaliophobia – the fear of long words; ironically, the word for the phobia is extremely long
- Homichlophobia – the fear of fog
- Geniophobia – the fear of chins
- Coulrophobia – the fear of clowns
- Vitrinophobia – the fear of glass
- Panphobia – the fear of everything

- Chromophobia – the fear of colors
- Aerophobia – the fear of flying
- Turophobia – the fear of cheese
- Anthophobia – the fear of flowers
- Ergophobia – the fear of working
- Astraphobia – the fear of thunder and lightning
- Aquaphobia – the fear of water
- Ephebiphobia – the fear of teenagers
- Genuphobia – the fear of knees
- Onomatophobia – the fear of names
- Pogonophobia – the fear of beards

Some are more easily understandable as fears than others, and the list contains some fears that many will find almost silly. But it's important to remember that these specific phobias can have a dramatic effect on people's lives.

9. What happens to people with phobias?

When someone has a phobia, their feeling of *flight or fight* becomes extremely reactive. They can experience something called a 'panic attack,' which makes it difficult to remain calm, and they can feel extremely scared.

Sometimes people with phobias may not be able to move properly due to their fear or may struggle to communicate normally. Panic attacks can also make people feel as if they're in imminent danger, to the point where they might even feel in pain!

So, it's important to be careful with people's phobias and make sure we avoid triggering them. It's a bit more serious than a little fright!

10. How to help people with phobias

This is an important part of this chapter. Phobias are quite common and if your friends or family members come into contact with a phobia, you want to make sure that you can help them.

The first thing is to try to remove potential phobias from our loved ones. If they're phobic about spiders and you see one, quickly remove it from the room. If they don't like the dark, make sure you turn the light on at nighttime. Simple steps like these are often exceptionally helpful in stopping them from even experiencing their phobia.

If they're unlucky and do come into contact with their phobia, then make sure you're calm with them and reassure them. Sometimes people just need to have someone acting super chilled out to help them. Once you're doing this, keep them safe and try to remove them from the phobia.

With the massive amount of information in this chapter, you can keep your loved ones safe from phobias. You can educate your friends and families about how serious they can be, even if they're also really fascinating and sometimes a bit strange. Remember that not everyone has a phobia, and many of us use the phrase when actually we mean 'I'm a bit scared of...' It's normal to be scared of things, but it doesn't necessarily mean you have a phobia just because spiders are a bit creepy.

THE WORLD'S STRANGEST DELICACIES

Are you aware that humans have about 10,000 taste buds in their mouths? Taste buds are mainly found on your tongue, but there are some on the roof of your mouth and throat as well. Taste buds are small, sensitive bumps that detect the taste of something. They detect five basic taste qualities: sweet, sour, savory, bitter, and salty. Your thousands of taste buds work together with your brain to detect how a food tastes and then figure out if that taste is pleasurable and safe to eat.

Ten thousand may sound like a lot of buds, but it's not that many compared to some animals. In fact, for some animals, their ability to taste can be the difference between life and death!

Catfish have over 175,000 taste buds in their mouths! They can taste their next meal from over a mile away underwater, so they can get to it first before other fish try to snaffle it. Cows have 25,000 taste buds in their mouths, so they can tell which vegetation and plants are poisonous. Dogs have only 1,700 taste buds. This is so they can quickly wolf down their meal without much tasting before other dogs in the litter get to it! It's a dog-eat-food-eat-dog world out there!

Humans can eat all kinds of different foods, which means we need to be able to detect a variety of things when we eat. Your childhood, family, friends, and birthplace can all have a big impact on what you like to taste, so 'food' can be very different across the world!

Here are some strange, and apparently yummy, foods that can be found across the globe, in the present day and back in our history. Afterwards, why not rank your top and bottom five dishes, or perhaps ask your parents to make them for you?

1. Hákarl

This food isn't for everyone, and many people who try it end up being sick from the overpowering taste! Hákarl is Iceland's national dish and is popular among some locals who like to laugh at all the enthusiastic tourists who fail to keep the food in their stomachs.

To make this dish, a shark is caught by a fisherman before being buried underneath stones for two to three months. Then it is recovered, before being hung out to dry in a shed for the same time again. The resulting portions of well-rotten shark are tinned before eating. The smell is overpoweringly hideous, and most people won't be able to eat the dish because of it. It's easy to imagine why: imagine the worst fish smell possible, then times it by 1,000.

2. Casu Marzu

Be prepared for this really disgusting addition to the world of food from Italy. The words 'Casu Marzu' translates to *rotten cheese*.

It's worth pointing out that this dish is now illegal to serve due to several health reasons. As you read, ask yourself if you'd ever be brave enough to try this revolting dish.

The cheese is made from two key ingredients: sheep's milk and maggots. Yup, maggots. The maggots are the larval (baby) stage of the cheese fly, which sit in the cheese and set about munching away at it. The horrid maggots help to ferment the cheese, break down some of the fats within it, and introduce a very soft texture to the cheese.

Supposedly the cheese 'goes off' (whatever that means) if the maggots aren't kept alive, so they aren't to be killed until consumption. At that point, the unlucky diner will spread the cheese on the bread and make sure the maggots die. If they don't, then you'll eat live maggots, which will cause a great deal of pain as the food is digested.

Absolutely disgusting - no wonder it's been banned! But Sardinian residents still eat this illegal cheese!

3. Haggis

If you ask a Scottish person what haggis is, then they may very well tell you a tale of a small, round animal. The animal has shorter left legs than right legs, so can sprint around steep hills without falling over. They're very fast and difficult to catch.

Unfortunately, that is a complete lie. There's no such animal as a haggis, but it is a national dish of Scotland and is often eaten at special events such as Burns Night in January of every year.

If a Haggis is plonked in front of you, it'll look like a light-brown ball, served with potatoes and vegetables. When cut into, a variety of spiced meat will tumble out and a sauce or gravy will be dribbled over the top. Sounds normal enough, right?

Well, all that meat is what is called offal. Offal is ground-up organs such as the heart, liver, and lungs, which are cooked with onions and pepper. The reason it's in a ball shape is that they have stuffed the offal into the stomach lining of a sheep and boiled it.

It sounds quite unpleasant. But if you can get past the whole 'organs' thing, then you might find a dish that's surprisingly flavorful and can provide some health benefits. Sometimes it is served "fried" and is said to be tasty.

Just don't say yes to 'a haggis hunt,' or you won't have any supper that evening.

4. Skewered scorpions

Picture a scorpion, with its pincers, stinging tail, and armored shell. Do you want to pop it in your mouth? No, probably not. But if you are to peruse the stalls at a food market in Beijing, China, you very well may see that very opportunity on offer.

Of course, one can't just eat any old scorpion. Some are venomous and could cause serious health problems if eaten. The Black Asian Forest Scorpion tends to be favored and is one of the few edible species.

The (dead) scorpions are first skewered on a stick, like a stingy kebab, and fried lightly for approximately a minute to cook the meat. They're then set aside for the day and re-fried for two minutes when a lucky customer orders a skewer before being seasoned with pepper and salt.

The scorpions remain a bit of a delicacy in parts of China and many tour guides will encourage you to try them if you find yourself in the food markets there...if you're brave enough!

5. Fugu

How do you want to feel when you eat your dinner? Many of us would opt for words such as "happy," "comfortable," and "safe." Unfortunately, if you indulge in the dish Fugu, that may not be guaranteed.

Fugu can be found in several East Asian countries such as Korea, Japan, and China. The dish is fish, quite simply. The fish is a puffer fish, the type that inflates itself into a big globe when they're scared. The thing is, it's exceptionally poisonous and could kill you.

There exists a toxin in the fish, that is lethal if consumed, which is why it can only be prepared by certain chefs. The chefs have to have worked for many years with the fish to prove that they can properly prepare it so that the dish doesn't end up killing someone. Even then, every year, people die from trying the fish when prepared by amateurs.

The fish is apparently quite a boring flavor, which begs the question, "Why risk your life to try a boring dish?" Perhaps it's the risk that makes it worth it. Either way, it's probably safer to stick with cod.

6. Here's looking at you, kid

There's something very creepy about eating something that could be looking right back at you.

In Japan, this doesn't seem to be such a worry as Maguro no Medama can be found on many menus and street food stands.

Japan is known for its excellent food. We think of sushi, ramen noodles, Kobe beef, and curries in their arsenal of amazing grub! If a server asked you if you'd like one of these dishes or a fish's eyeballs, you'd likely ask them to please leave you alone and never talk to you again. But this is something that you can have if you'd like to - Maguro no Medama, the eyeball of the tuna fish.

Tuna is a popular fish the world over and, in Japan, the tuna is highly valued. As such, they have no desire to waste any of it. Chefs can prepare the eyeball in a few ways, such as steamed, fried, boiled, or raw. It doesn't matter how you prepare it, though, it's still a gross eyeball.

If you're ever in Japan and feel like you'd be missing out without this gelatinous, flavorless gloop, then find your way to a fish market and keep your eye out for an eye out.

7. Cheese in a can

In some parts of Europe, cheese is an art. In England, the town of Cheddar gave its name to the most common cheese in the world (cheddar cheese), while the official Parmesan cheese (Parmigiano Reggiano) can only be made in a specific part of Italy. In other words, it's taken seriously.

This means that about 50% of the world who enjoy real, delicious cheese are left confused as citizens of the United States of America enjoy *squirty cheese* or *cheese in a can.*

This foodstuff is really quite strange, and many North Americans are shocked to learn that it isn't found in many shops elsewhere in the world. Italians take cheese very seriously and would scoff at the mere mention of the product (on their way to eat the maggoty cheese from earlier).

The food is a compressed can of liquid 'cheese,' which can be squirted onto...whatever you want. To call the product 'cheese' is also a bit of a stretch; many people claim that it isn't really cheese at all, but millions of Americans swear by the stuff!

8. Rocky Mountain Oysters

An uncommon delicacy that also hails from the great U S of A is the delicious-*looking* Rocky Mountain Oysters. Oysters are expensive, delicious seafood enjoyed all over the world, with customers paying outrageous money to sample a mere few.

However, Rocky Mountain Oysters aren't oysters at all; in fact, they're something far grosser.

They're bull's testicles.

If you're not sure what that is, it's part of the 'private areas' of a male cow. The product is sometimes also known as 'prairie oysters' and is enjoyed regularly in areas of Canada, the USA, and Argentina. The 'oysters' are deep-fried in oil and seasoned, and they resemble pretty much any other deep-fried food you can think of.

You can locate the bizarre appetizer at baseball games and special festivals dedicated to the product in America. You tend to find the food in an area where there is a lot of cattle farming, as that is where the strange (and let's face it, gross-sounding) product is most frequent.

If you're visiting America or relatives in Illinois, be wary if they ask you to try a prairie oyster.

9. Cuy

The guinea pig is such an adorable animal, isn't it? They're large enough to be given a small cuddle, as furry as a hamster, and they squeak like a small puppy! Millions of kids across the world want one as a pet (even if they can be quite annoying), while many adults in South America want one with a side of rice.

That's right, in countries such as Peru, Columbia, Ecuador, and Bolivia, the guinea pig is a traditional delicacy. That may sound a bit sad, but there are plenty of sensible reasons for them to feature on menus.

The guinea pig is a very common animal in South America; in fact, there are tens of millions of them! Guinea pigs breed quite happily, so the numbers are sustainable, and they exist as food in the food chains of many predators. Eagles, wolves, snakes, and coyotes all dine on the little fur-balls, so why not humans?

They're supposedly rather tasty, once you get past the 'pet' aspect of it, and they're usually served as a main course, though you may need to have more than one.

Remember not to ask for 'fries with that' when you're at the pet store, though. The cashiers don't like it.

10. Llama brain

It's difficult to pretend that this course isn't gross. We are once again in South America, this time in Bolivia.

The llama is a useful animal in Bolivia. Llamas are also favorites of tourists, who like to walk them, play with them, and ride carts pulled by them. They're friendly and have interesting personalities, making them a bit of a moneymaker. When they're not interacting with people, farmers shear llamas for their wool, which is high quality and strong. When they're not being shorn for their sheep, nor hanging with tourists, they are killed for meat.

Bolivians hate to waste food, especially when it has come from an animal such as the llama. So, they make sure to eat all of it...

all of it. So, as well as indulging in llama steaks and llama stew, you can also sample llama brain.

Brains are prepared in a variety of ways, such as poaching and frying, but the end result is very much still a brain. Reports suggest that the sensation of brain-munching is creamy and not much like eating meat at all. It has a savory flavor and is slightly buttery.

Put your mind to it (get it?): Do you think that you'd be able to consume the wrinkly grey matter?

So, there you have it! A selection of strange, disgusting, and intriguing delicacies from around the world. Isn't it interesting that we don't all agree on what 'gross' is? If you're from Cambodia, you may enjoy crunching down a tarantula but would find the idea of cheese in a can revolting. While a Scottish person would consume the innards of a sheep but not the legs of a little frog!

How different we all are. There are hundreds more strange, bizarre, and gag-inducing meals out there, and the best way to experience them is to try them! It's worth asking yourself whether you'd give these snacks and gourmet-puke-encouragers a try if you had them in front of you.

Make sure to tell your friends and family about this revolting little collection that you've just read about, and see what you can get them to agree to eat. If anyone says that they'll eat the Casu Marzu, then they're disgusting, and make sure to tell them so.

BAFFLING INVENTIONS AND CONFUSING INVENTORS

Have you ever stopped to consider that almost everything you see in your day has been invented? As in, someone made it. When you watch TV, someone (or many people) spends hours of their lives perfecting an understanding of technology to make that particular TV. The fork you hold when you eat dinner? Well, someone over 2,500 years ago designed a fork, and we still use it now.

The point is that everything that isn't from nature was invented by an inventor, and it is amazing how many inventions and inventors there have been.

But for every fork and TV, the useful inventions, there are many inventions that clever inventors have spent hours of their lives creating, but they remain completely useless or just plain bizarre. Have a read of some of the strangest and most mind-bogglingly useless inventions that have ever been conceived.

Note: You are encouraged to google these designs, as there are illustrations that accompany them that may help bring them to life!

1. Samuel S. Applegate's "Device For Waking Persons From Sleep" (1882)

Many of us wish that we could get up earlier. Well, actually more of us wish that we didn't have to get up at all. But if we have to get up, we'd like to get up at the right time and in the best way possible, right?

Well in 1882, over a hundred years after someone had already made the alarm clock, Samuel S. Applegate created and copyrighted the "Device for waking persons from sleep." You'll agree it sounds genius, but perhaps it'd be best to buy one for your worst enemy.

The device sits above your bed and is rigged to a clock. An alarm clock, in fact. When the alarm goes off (which wakes you up), the device kicks in. It releases a basket full of wood onto your face to "cause pain" for the sleeper.

It sounds ridiculous, but try and argue that you wouldn't be awake after that! If you want to simulate this experience, ask your younger brother or sister to simply walk into your bedroom at 7 a.m. and punch you in the face. Guaranteed, you'll be up and raring to go after that.

2. Charles G. Purdy's "Head Exerciser" (1923)

Do you ever wish that your head was in better shape? No, no one does.

But that thought didn't cross Charles G. Purdy's mind in 1923 when he decided to make a device that would help you exercise by using your head. You can't do this on your own; you'll need a partner. You could also do this with a piece of bungee cord if you fancy head-butting someone really, really hard.

The device is a stick that has two metal plates at either end. The metal plates go into the mouths of the idiots - sorry, the customers - that bought the product. At this point, you should be staring into the eyes of your friend with a bit of metal in your mouth and thinking "What on earth are we doing, this is ridiculous?"

Together you each pull the stick in opposite directions using your mouth. The stick is loaded with springs, so it will constantly try to do the opposing action to what you're doing. It's a tug-of-war with your mouth and teeth.

We don't know if anyone ever bought one of these. Most people probably thought they could do without exercising their heads, knocking out their friends, and losing their teeth.

3. David Kendrick's "Life Expectancy Timepiece" (1991)

There's that old question that people like to ask: "If you could find out exactly when you were going to die, would you want to know?" People are always split! If you say yes, then you'll know how long you have left but also will be constantly counting down to that day. If you reply no, then you don't know when it'll happen and run the risk of wasting time. Either way, there's no way you can find that out anyway, right?

Well, David Kendrick attempted to do just that.

He created a nifty little wristwatch that would present a perfect countdown toward the precise second of your death. There aren't tons of information on exactly *how* this works, but you put in some data or information, and it works out the countdown.

There's probably a reason that the product was never sold. Why would anyone want to walk around with a constant countdown of when they'll expire on their wrist? Also, it definitely didn't work.

It's always better to respond "no" to that question.

4. K. Lange's "Double Bicycle" (1905)

When you read about this invention, stop and google it. Then stop again and think about how much better BMX biking would be if riders used these instead of the normal bikes.

Have you always aspired to do a forward roll on your bicycle without even a bit of effort? This doesn't mean a front flip, but a *roll*. Well, the Double Bicycle is for you. It was specifically created "for looping the loop."

The Double Bicycle is like stacking a bicycle on top of another bicycle. This way you have four wheels, two above and two below, with you sat in the middle and hunched over. When you apply the brake and lean forward, the bicycle will roll over itself, and all of your friends will cheer and applaud.

It sounds just a bit crazy, but you'll be the envy of everyone at the skate park the moment you start rolling this bad boy up and down a halfpipe! Now available, only twice the price of a normal bike and half as useful.

5. P. Plant's "Cork Swimming Suit" (1882)

Nowadays when you visit the beach or swimming pool, the swimming costumes/bathing suits/trunks/beachwear that are worn are designed for two purposes.

1) To be functional for swimming.
2) For fashion.

What P. Plant managed to do in 1882 was design a swimming suit that does neither.

In 1882, people wouldn't wear the same outfits we do today. Swimming suits covered most of the body, as in those days it was rude to show too much at the pool. P. Plant saw these suits and thought that they didn't make swimming easier; in fact, many costumes made it more difficult.

Plant's suit was entirely made of cork, a very light wooden material. The body would be completely covered by it, and it was meant to allow for "perfectly free motions of the body and limbs." The cork would help you float on water and allow you to easily swim on by your jealous colleagues in their stupid old-fashioned costumes.

Of course, after wearing the suit more than twice, the cork would begin to become useless and the costume could dissolve in front of your very eyes, leaving you a bit more "perfectly free" than you at first wished.

6. Lucy Barmby's "Anti-Eating Face Mask" (1980)

You know how when you go out to a restaurant, and the servers are constantly eating your food before it even gets to your table? No? Well, that's because they don't, and it's not a problem that anyone has ever thought about before.

That is, other than Lucy Barmby. In 1980 she created a mask that would strap over someone's mouth, making it impossible to eat food. It was designed specifically to stop chefs and servers pinching from people's plates on the way to their tables, and even came with a padlock! (Just make sure you don't lose the key)

This invention is so bizarre as it tackles a problem that doesn't exist. If they are hungry, the chefs and servers are unlikely to take food from your plate because they work in an enormous kitchen. If they want to eat some food, then they'll cook themselves some food and eat that.

Plus, how creepy would it look if you're trying to chow down on a plate of fries and your waiters are walking around with metal masks over their mouths? Weird!

7. Eric D. Page's "Forehead Support Apparatus" (2004)

This invention might exclude any readers that don't sometimes stand when they visit the bathroom, but you'll be able to get the gist!

In some lavatories, there are things called urinals. The urinal is essentially a trough or small area where one stands and relieves oneself. They save some room and get people in and out quicker.

What gets difficult is keeping your head upright when you're doing this. Or at least, this is what Eric Page thought was a difficulty in his life. That's why he invented his Forehead Support Apparatus, which is basically a headrest that sits above the urinal. The visitor then leans their head against it, which improves their life in no way.

It's not difficult to see why this didn't catch on. Why do lavatories need people leaning against the wall while they go to the bathroom? Surely, they should just focus on the job at hand and make sure they do that correctly?

So, while Eric Page may have a headrest above his lavatory, you won't see one in any public bathroom near you.

8. Nicole M. Dubus' "Fork With Timer" (1995)

In the 1990s, everyone was in a rush. Either to go to work, go on holiday, sit down, or just finish their dinner. Or that's what Nicole Dubus thought when she created the product that no one on Earth needed - called "Fork With Timer."

How much do you need to explain? Picture a fork (well done on doing that). Now, in your mind, put a small digital timer into the handle of that fork. Congratulations on picturing the "Fork With Timer."

Dubus' invention is very simple, and sometimes the most genius inventions are the simplest ones. Unfortunately, she's created something without any use. Why do you need to time yourself when you eat, and why wouldn't you just use a clock or watch to do that?

These questions didn't pop into Nicole Dubus' head when she copyrighted the invention, and it didn't become an instant success. Back to the drawing board for her then.

What next? A spoon with a pen in it?

9. Chris T. Michael's "Tv Control Device" (1976)

Before the days of remote controls, adjusting your television meant that you had to physically get up and go to the set. Be it for changing the channel (of which there were about three), adjusting the volume, or even just turning it on had to be done physically with your hands.

You'd think that this is what drove Chris T. Michael to invent the "TV Control Device," a large stick that helped you turn the dials and press buttons on the set from your armchair. But that can't have been the case because the remote control had already been invented by 1976, so why on Earth would anyone need a long stick in their living room?

Chris' reasons were that the stick comes in different lengths, is cheaper to buy than a remote control, and won't get lost as easily. True, Chris, but also it will cause every friend who visits you to say, "Why on Earth have you got a huge stick in your living room?"

10. Alva K. Dawson's "Combined Head-Covering and Hair-Comb" (1920)

The name isn't very catchy; perhaps "CombyCap" would work better, or even "CappyComb."

Alva Dawson designed this product to help remove the frustration of "hat hair." Hat hair is when you put a hat on and, as it shifts about throughout the day, it ruins your hairstyle. This is annoying for some, and a real pain for others. Most people might be tempted either to not wear a hat or to bring something with them to style their hair after wearing the hat, like a comb.

But Alva thought, "What if those were combined?" This would only work for quite short hair, which you comb back across your head. As you remove the cap from your head, the comb pushes back through your hair, ensuring that it's slick and combed even after cycling!

The problem, of course, is that this wouldn't work all the time. The comb could become stuck or break, and not every customer has hair that needs combing back. It's also quite uncomfortable to have a comb pressing against your head all day, so it really did more harm than good.

Maybe it's easier to just carry a small bag with hair adjustment products if you're that worried.

This brings our chapter on inventions to a strange close. Every invention mentioned here is completely and utterly true; they were all thought up and copyrighted by their hilarious inventors!

You can investigate these more and find some other strange products for yourself. There are things called 'patents' that people buy, to register their idea as being theirs and to make sure it doesn't get copied by anyone. You can search for more of these using Google, which has an archive of patents. Be warned, however; there are millions of them, and many of them are quite sensible and not particularly fun.

These people have inserted their names into the history books with their strange inventions, so anyone can do it! Why not have a go at coming up with some interesting, quirky, and less useless designs yourself?

THE AMAZING ANIMAL OLYMPICS

Welcome to the incredible, world-class, definitive Animal Olympics! Here, animals from across the diverse and vast kingdom will compete for gold, silver, and bronze medals in our chosen Olympic sports!

In this chapter, we'll be challenging the animal kingdom to a series of Olympic sports to see who comes out on top, and who is scrambling around for Bronze. You'll hear of the world's fastest, strongest, and best jumpers and the most amazing marathon runners that are all battling it out for a spot on the podium!

Enjoy the world's best spectacle, the Animal Olympics!

1. 100m Sprint

Event: The 100m sprint is a test of pure speed. Who can run 100m (109.36 yards) the quickest? The fastest human to have ever run the 100m sprint was Usain Bolt, who ran the full length in 9.58 seconds. How does the rest of the animal kingdom get on?

Bronze: Third place goes to the quarter horse! The quarter horse is a breed of horse that remains the most popular in America. It's named the quarter horse because of the speed at which it can run a quarter of a mile.

When this thing gets going, it scores a time of 4.09 seconds.

Silver: Second goes to the pronghorn, and it's no surprise given that it is the fastest land mammal in the Western Hemisphere. It looks a bit like an antelope with big, curved antlers and can run 55 miles per hour for a sustained period.

The Pronghorn takes the silver medal with a time of 4.06 seconds.

Gold: First place, the gold medal, and all the meat you can eat will go to…, the cheetah! For any animal buff, they would have seen this coming. This competition was made for the cheetah, the sleek and powerful big cat that lives in Africa. The cheetah is the fastest land animal on Earth, somehow running at 75 mph, though only over short distances. But that's all it needs for the 100m sprint.

The cheetah absolutely destroys the competition with a time of 2.98 seconds!!

Honorable Mention: A quick honorable mention goes to the peregrine falcon. This bird of prey uses inconceivable speed to catch its food, but it's disqualified from the 100m sprint. Firstly, because flying is cheating, and secondly because it uses gravity to pick up speed, which is also cheating. Still, it can reach speeds of 198 mph and would have a competitive time of 1.1 seconds.

2. Weightlifting

Event: The weightlifting event is all about brute strength. Who can lift the heaviest thing? Of course, this can be a bit unfair as an event because some animals are far bigger than others, so will have the advantage. So, the judges will consider animals of all sizes and decide who is the most physically impressive.

Bronze: Proudly receiving the bronze, and bringing some pride back to the herd, is the elephant.

Elephants are impressive, let's face it. Remarkably intelligent, enormous, and exceptionally strong to boot, they can lift more than any other animal on land. An elephant's trunk is basically a long tube of strong muscle, and it can use this to lift seven tons. That is about as heavy as a 48-foot-long truck that you might see on the highway.

Well done to Nelly, who packed her trunk with seven tons of food, and said hello to the bronze award!

Silver: In the second place, receiving a lot of applause and some fish in the name of freedom, is the eagle.

Eagles are a group in the category of 'birds of prey,' and use the laws of physics to help them catch their food. They take the silver today because of their ability to carry animals that are four times their size, hundreds of yards into the air. Other ground animals are only lifting their weights a tiny bit off of the ground; the eagle is performing one heck of a lift!

Gold: Finally, the gold medal for the world's strongest animal goes to the amazing, incredible... *dung beetle!*

Yes, it would be squished into a paste by the elephant, but its weightlifting is incredibly impressive. The dung beetle is a small creature, no more than an inch long, but it's able to lift 1,141 times its own bodyweight! If a person could do that, that would be like lifting six full double-decker buses by themselves!

No animal comes close to the dung beetle in terms of lifting compared to its own body weight, and it happily takes home the gold.

3. Boxing

Event: Boxing is fighting. The athletes in this competition are all about being ferocious, aggressive, and winning their fights. The best human boxer at the Olympics was László Papp, who took home three gold medals during his time as an Olympian. However, that was only against other humans...

Bronze: Third place goes to the animal that could actually get into a boxing ring and give a convincing performance. That animal is the kangaroo.

Kangaroos are quite adorable for many reasons, but don't let that fool you. Kangaroos have been known to get into physical fights with humans. They stand upright, using their tail for balance, and swing with jabs from the left, then the right, two lefts, followed by a left, and finally a right. If that doesn't get you, they can use their powerful legs to kick out - breaking bones when they do so. They can literally kickbox!

The kangaroo wouldn't always win in boxing, but it wouldn't get thrown out for disobeying the rules! As such, it gets the bronze.

Silver: The following animal is not a land animal, and it would struggle to participate in a round of real boxing. But it takes the silver for being the undisputed champion in the ocean, and that is the great white shark.

The great white shark is a remarkably efficient predator, able to smell its prey from 3.1 miles away and have the speed to get there in a matter of minutes. They're found in almost every ocean and are always at the top of the food chain.

Nothing stands a chance when coming up against a great white, and it takes second place. It only loses out on gold because it can't get into the ring.

Gold: Our best boxer goes to an animal that is so ferocious and aggressive, that it's officially recognized as "the world's most fearless animal" by the *Guinness World Records*. That animal is the honey badger.

That may be the cutest name of all time, but this small, black-and-white omnivore has an aggressive side almost unmatched. The honey badger is well known for attacking anything. They're known to fight lions, take bites out of horses, and eat the venomous king cobra. Over time, they've evolved to eat anything too, and can even digest bone!

Without a doubt, the honey badger brings a level of ferocity to the ring that no other can match, and it deservedly takes the gold.

4. Diving

Event: The diving event is all about who can sink into the water the quickest and the deepest. Normally, in the human event, points are given for style and elegance. We'll do the same here, but unfortunately, our animal competitors have told me they don't care about style and elegance.

Bronze: The bronze award is given to an animal that doesn't live *in* the ocean. Therefore, its diving abilities are all the more impressive given that it starts on land. That animal is the *emperor penguin.*

Emperor penguins mainly eat fish, but they also enjoy deeper-dwelling creatures. The penguin will happily dive to a depth of 585 yards to gobble up unlucky squids, and so takes third place.

Silver: Silver has been awarded to an animal that can grow to be almost 22 yards long and holds the record for the predators with the largest teeth. A round of applause, please, for the sperm whale.

The sperm whale is a vast animal, and they are rarely on the receiving end of hunting in the ocean. They dive to extreme depths to catch squid and will lower themselves to depths of 2460 yards in order to find them. An incredible feat, no doubt, eclipsed only by...

Gold: The Cuvier's beaked whale! We award the gold to the beaked whale, and everyone stands to applaud before shouting, "I don't know what that looks like!"

The beaked whale looks like a cross between a dolphin and a whale and holds the world record for the deepest dive *ever* recorded. Before they dive, these whales exhale and have negative buoyancy. They sink quickly and search for their prey at depths of 3,272 yards, blowing the competition out of the water! Congratulations to the beaked whale!

5. Swimming

Event: Swimming is all about…well, swimming. Swimming is something that humans are generally a bit rubbish at. It's not that we're lazy; we're just not aquatic animals. We possess the ability to swim, but we don't need to be excellent at it. Gold-medalist Michael Phelps set a record for swimming 200 meters (218.72 yards) in 1.42 minutes, which sets him at 4.7 mph. How will he stack up against the quickest, best swimmers in the ocean?

Bronze: Third place is gallantly won by an animal that many have forgotten exists outside of a can. That animal is the yellowfin tuna.

This tuna is set apart from other tuna due to its distinctive yellow fins and striped belly. Most people don't know that tuna are huge fish, reaching weights of approximately 400 lbs. Their size and weight make the fish seem as if it couldn't be particularly fast, but the yellowfin reaches speeds of 50 mph in the open ocean - yes, that's right, 50!

Congratulations to the yellowfin who sneaks into third but stands no chance against second and first place.

Silver: The fastest fish in the ocean belongs to one category called the billfish, and they will be taking silver and gold. The billfish are recognized by their long protruding nose and rapid speed. The billfish's most famous family member is the swordfish and that is who takes second place today.

The swordfish is agile, heavy, and found in the Atlantic and Pacific oceans. Weighing in at nearly 1,200 lbs. with a long, sharp nose, these sub-aquatic jousters are not to be messed with. They're able to top speeds of 60 mph and can use that speed to jump out of the ocean for some fantastic photo opportunities.

Well done to the swordfish, but its close relative is still far out in front.

Gold: First place, topping the swordfish's excellent 60 mph, is its long-lost cousin, the sailfish.

The sailfish is smaller than the swordfish, though looks quite similar. They usually weigh only 180 lbs. and this might help them in gaining a little bit more speed through the water. The sailfish uses its long bill to slash at its prey, which it can take apart in seconds. It tops an unbelievable 68 mph and far outstrips the other competitors, including Michael Phelps.

Well done to the sailfish. The 200m freestyle is truly a 'blink and you'll miss it' race in the animal kingdom.

Honorable Mention: An honorable mention belongs to yet another billfish. This one's called the black marlin. The black marlin is far slower than our other competitors, as it's only been clocked at 22 mph by scientists. But one fisherman claims that he attempted to catch one and recorded it traveling at 82 mph!

If that story is true, then the black marlin would be the fastest fish in the ocean, for sure - but no scientist has been able to confirm it. Perhaps it was just one very fast fish? Or maybe the fisherman was lying?

6. Marathon

Event: The marathon is an extra-long race, with a distance of 26.2 miles. It's exceptionally difficult to do, but humans across the planet love training themselves to go the distance in front of their friends and families. How does the animal kingdom compare, however? And who will come out on top in this competition?

Bronze: Third place goes to an animal that has aided human beings in deserts across the world for thousands of years. Though they may not look like much, the camel easily takes the third place today!

Camels are specially adapted to withstand the harsh climate of the desert. They store food and water within their humps, enabling them to keep up their energy levels - and they can run quickly, too!

Camels can hold a consistent run of 25 mph for a long time, sometimes reaching 40. They complete the marathon in one hour and two minutes and deservedly take the bronze medal home with them. Not just a pretty face then!

Silver: There isn't much between second and first place, so the recipient of the silver medal may well feel like they've been cheated! That would be fair enough, but they can take second place with grace and decorum. Please stand and applaud the pronghorn antelope!

The antelope is a master of stamina and can achieve extremely fast speeds for hours. This is necessary so that they can escape predators, and when that predator could well be a cheetah, you can see why they're built this way. The antelope achieves an average speed of 30 mph and can top 55 mph when it really feels like it.

As a result, the pronghorn antelope takes the silver medal with a marathon time of about 45 minutes.

Gold: We did say that it was going to be a close one, so close in fact that the winner of the gold medal also finished with a time of 45 minutes. Our glorious victor in the marathon event is the ostrich.

The ostrich is built for endurance because of the way its legs are designed. Their legs are made up of tendons, which act as a spring. When they land on their foot, they almost instantly pop back up, using very little energy to do so. Because of this, their legs are very light, and help them maintain speeds of 30 mph for incredible distances. Though the antelope may beat them in a sprint (as ostriches can only achieve 50 mph), the ostrich would be able to run for longer.

Well done to the ostrich, who takes the gold for a 45-minute marathon!

7. High Jump

Event: The high jump is a fun event. In human events, a horizontal stick is suspended in the air and the athletes have to jump over it. Whoever can jump over the highest stick wins. Humans are decent jumpers when trained, but how will we compare to the rest of the kingdom? For this event, we'll be considering how high an animal jumps when compared to its own size. A human can barely jump twice their own height.

Bronze: Achieving a valiant and impressive bronze medal is a surprising entry from the ocean. Third place goes to the dolphin!

Dolphins are well known for their intelligence and connection with humans, with thousands of tourists looking to swim with them every year. But their ability to jump is exceptionally impressive. Dolphins can project themselves out of the ocean, reaching a height between 15 and 30 feet. That's the equivalent of a human being jumping over a two-story house!

The dolphins represent the aquatic mammals in a competition in which most wouldn't have thought they'd have a chance. For the next medals, we look to some smaller creatures.

Silver: Achieving a comfortable second place today, much to the unhappiness of the arachnophobes, is the jumping spider.

Many humans hate spiders, either fearing their bite or slightly creepy look. If you ever feel the need to persuade someone not to despise them so much, then it may be worth showing them the jumping spider. This spider is tiny and would fit on your pinky fingernail with room to spare. They're quite curious and some people keep them as tiny pets!

Watch out for their jump, however, as from a standing position, the spider can jump up to 100 times their size. That's like a human jumping the length of two soccer pitches in one go!

Gold: The gold medal is awarded to an animal you probably can't see from where you're sitting right now. If you produce a magnifying glass, however, you'll be able to spot the humble but excellent flea.

Fleas are 0.2 inches long, and miniscule in size. If you own a dog, you may sometimes spot them hopping around your pooch's fur, which can be annoying. But they're amazing jumpers and are by far the best in the world.

The flea jumps 200 times its own body length with no run-up, utilizing its spring-like legs to ping into the air. If we could jump that far and high, we'd be able to jump over the Empire State Building.

Next time you spot a flea, give it a small round of applause for being the world's best!

8. Acrobatics

Event: The acrobatics events are about gymnastic achievement. This includes amazing balancing acts, showing grip strength, and somersaults to make your head spin. Judging this event usually involves judges who know everything about the discipline and whether someone is doing it well or not. The animals will be judged in the same way, not using statistics and numbers, but considering their grace and ability in acrobatics.

Bronze: The bronze award goes to an animal that may surprise you, as it doesn't *seem* particularly graceful. However, it's designed to contort itself, to show astounding flexibility, and even the occasional somersault. That animal is the octopus.

Octopi don't have bones but do have soft and flexible skin. This means that an octopus can force itself through virtually any gap it finds. For this reason, they're difficult to keep in captivity and can escape from aquariums with ease. The octopus is graceful as it floats through the ocean, but it all comes down to its flexibility, which wins it the bronze medal.

Silver: Our second-placed acrobat is a lumbering giant ape, with spectacular acrobatic technique and a glorious coat to boot! Our silver medalist is the orangutan.

Orangutans are big old apes, with the males weighing in at 191 lbs. Their distinctive orange fur drapes across their body, and their flat head gives them a mysterious look. But more than that, they are fantastic gymnasts. They're native to the forests of

Borneo and Sumatra and use their enormous arms to swing from trees, find food, and carry objects.

The orangutan glides through the trees with effortless poise, their glorious ginger hair swishing through the breeze. With their hand grip keeping them steady, they climb trees like humans climb a ladder. The orangutan takes second place, and the judges applaud their remarkable grace.

Gold: Finally, we get to the ultimate prize for the most graceful, agile, acrobatic animal of them all (according to the judges). Today, the gold medal goes to the cat!

Cats are found as pets all over the world and have been in that position for thousands of years. You'd assume that over all that time, they'd become used to being waited on hand and paw, but no! Cats are gifted with extreme flexibility and sharp reflexes that give them the prize today.

Cats possess cushioning disks between the vertebrae in their spine, which help them absorb the impact of rough landings and twisting their bodies. It helps them remain flexible when they climb and jump, leading to them looking like graceful dancers as they expertly glide through our homes.

Congratulations, cats - Enjoy first place - why not celebrate with a nap?

9. Fencing/Javelin Throw/Shotput

Event: The following category is a combination of events, as we look at which animal best uses objects and weapons. When it comes to the use of tools and weapons, humans are unparalleled. Scientists estimate that one of the main reasons for humanity's dominance over the world is our ability to use things with our hands. So, out of fairness, humans are disqualified. This round will be about the animals who show their ability to use tools that would help them compete in the sports of fencing, javelin throwing, and shotput.

Bronze: Third place goes to a remarkable animal that shows its ability to duel with swords at a young age. This intelligent, fencing animal is the raven.

Ravens are known for their smarts, and this is on display early. Young ravens will break twigs off of trees to use as swords, and they fight each other!

The 'swords' are useless in an actual fight - their beaks are far sharper - but they enjoy playing with them and pretending to joust. As impressive as this is, the raven only achieves a bronze position because it's simply not taking the competition seriously, but congratulations for representing the birds in this round!

Silver: Next up, second place, and we're looking at an animal that can shotput as well as any human can. Winning their second medal in the Olympics is the elephant.

Elephants use their trunks to great advantage, as we saw in the weightlifting event. When they become irritated or bored, they can launch heavy rocks with startling accuracy. There have been many cases of people being on the receiving end of a flying boulder, which of course isn't a *good* thing, but it's impressive.

Elephants have also used rocks to down fences that they wish to pass through, showing an impressive level of intelligence. Due to their spectacular throwing ability, they take a well-deserved silver medal.

Gold: The gold medalist in this category isn't much of a surprise. Given their close relationship with humans, they are best equipped to impress in their ability to throw javelin-like objects. This animal is the chimpanzee.

Chimpanzees have shown the ability to make, use, and reuse spears. In particular, a group was documented in Senegal, showing us how they managed to get hold of some meat. The chimps sharpen sticks with their teeth before launching and prodding the spears at bush babies. They then pull them off the stick. Once they're done, they clean the spear and use it again.

As gross as it is, it's the best javelin throwing in the animal kingdom, and so the chimpanzee takes the gold medal in this section of the field events!

10. Breakdancing

Event: The last event of our Animal Olympics is Breakdancing. In Paris in 2024, it will be the first time that dancing is judged at the Olympics, as breakdancing is included. While humans have perfected, and invented, breakdancing, animals got there first when it comes to busting a move!

Let's see who comes off best in a competition of the shakers, movers, and steppers of the animal kingdom!

Bronze: Taking the third position is an animal that is collecting a second medal for its species at the games. The little guy with the big moves is the peacock spider, which is a form of jumping spider!

The peacock spider is a gorgeous, tiny arachnid. Its body is colored with reds, blues, and oranges in a vibrant display. When it attempts to attract a partner, the spider raises its miniature abdomen above its head and brings its front two legs to the sky. Then, it begins to shimmy from side to side, doing a rather beautiful tango dance.

It's an oddly adorable spectacle, given the spiders' size, but it's an important dance in the life cycle of the peacock spider. The dance can literally mean life or death; if the female isn't impressed, then she may eat the male dancer.

In recognition, the peacock spider takes bronze!

Silver: The competition hots up as a first medal is won for the dance troupe wearing black and yellow. The honeybee takes second!

You've probably seen bees bobbing around in the summer, and you might doubt that they could be graceful, never mind dancers. When a honeybee discovers a source of nectar, its job is to go and tell the others so they can collect as much as possible. So, the bee will zoom back into the hive and get everyone's attention. This is where the dance comes in.

Their celebratory dance is known as the 'waggle dance.' To do it, they form a figure-of-eight pattern while wiggling their abdomens and buzzing their wings. The hive becomes excited and takes notes (not literally!) on where the nectar is before setting off to gather more.

Because it is cute and surprising, the honeybee brings home the silver! When it gets home, it will probably do another little dance to tell the others about it.

Gold: When you think of an animal that does a spectacular dance, there is probably one that comes to mind above the small ones that have already won a medal. It's famous because it deserves it - the gold medal goes to the peacock.

Peacocks are large birds that are known for their magnificent plumage. The male peacock spreads out its stunning feathers in a captivating fan shape, before strutting around the female peacock. It shakes its tail feathers and spins around, demonstrating its ability on the dance floor.

If you see the dance, you'll struggle not to be enraptured by the sight. The feathers have a pattern that looks like several eyes, gazing back at you, making the peacock a godly vision. It's a gorgeous sight and wins the peacock a gold medal. Yet another for the birds!

Now comes the closing ceremony for the Animal Olympics. Flocks of birds would parade around the stadium, jeering at the primates who thump their chests, thrilled with their medal hauls. The fish proudly take ownership of the swimming pool, cackling at the pathetic humans who couldn't best them in anything.

All in all, a wonderful competition was had by all. It's a shame we couldn't cover more during the beloved event, but there'll be a new competition in another four years.

THE GADGETS OF THE FUTURE!

For the last few hundred years, there have been unceasing technological changes. The world we live in is so completely different from how it was 20 years ago, let alone 50! If you don't believe that, then go and find an old person and respectfully ask them what the biggest changes in their lives have been. Guaranteed they never would have imagined something as amazing as a smartphone, or the constant access to the internet, in their earlier years.

So, what is going to change over the course of your life that will define the future? What major inventions are potentially just around the corner that will leave you amazed as you sit in your retirement home? Here are a few major developments to keep your eye on. Which would you most like to have access to already?

1. Artificially intelligent deceased?

Artificial Intelligence (AI) has been in development for a long time, but it's improving rapidly. AI is used by media companies to create assistants to help you such as Siri or Alexa. Currently, they can help you book taxis, turn on lights, or order a takeaway. Imagine how much more they'll be capable of in another ten years.

Now you can use a website such as ChatGPT to write full essays for you, while our social media accounts can predict what we want to buy before we even know we're going to buy it! That's already incredible, and a little scary. So, where is this going?

According to Ray Kurzweil, a famous American computer scientist, AI is going to be used to help preserve our loved ones after they have passed. He says that companies are looking into the possibility of sending nanobots into the minds of people to extract their memories. Someone can then upload the nanobot to a robot or program and act like your friend or relative.

Creepy but impressive. You could have your friends available at the click of a button and communicate with a digital version of them. Is that a bit much, or a chance for a fun exchange with someone who's gone?

2. Space vacations

In the 1960s and 1970s, the expanse of space was being studied and visited by space corporations across the world. The first stop was to get into space, which was done time after time. Then the mission was to get to the moon, which was accomplished a few times by NASA. What next? Craft has made it to Mars, and there are plans for humans to go there soon as well. Meanwhile, super-rich people such as Richard Branson and Elon Musk have thought about space differently.

Many experts now think that it's going to be very likely that, within the next 30 to 40 years, you'll be able to take trips into space for your holidays.

How will this work? Well, it's going to be super, super expensive. Virgin was the first to market their space tourism, with tickets costing almost $300,000! That's without a guarantee it even works, and only for a few hours.

Still, imagine in the 2060s, paying a large fee to spend two weeks in a ginormous space shuttle, traveling around the solar system. You could visit the Moon and Mars, and never leave the longest cruise in the galaxy. The plan will be for the shuttles to have access to bars, restaurants, and amusements for the whole family. Though a lot of work is still to be done…

Currently, space travel is still a risky business, and many people have died during their journey into the endless darkness. As long as the companies planning for this venture can prove it's safe enough to do, then it will go ahead. Though it's a bit tricky, legally. After all, no one owns space. So, who can tell you what to do with it?

There's a lot of money in the idea, and if it becomes successful, it will be the most desirable holiday destination ever. The plan has its critics, however. Many have said that Hawaii is even better than the Moon. After all, there's not even a beach up there!

3. E-Skin

This idea might sound a bit bizarre, but the scientists who have developed the E-Skin think that it will help people remain better connected over the internet. Have you ever found yourself wishing you could hug someone who's hundreds of miles away? Perhaps your family member is having a hard time, or your friend has moved from where you live, leaving you desperate to reach out to them. Well, maybe you'll be able to before too long.

The E-Skin is a wearable product that is in development at the City University of Hong Kong. It's covered in careful sensors that measure your movements and convert them into electric signals. The movement is then sent to another E-Skin system, where they're turned into vibrations.

What this means is that, if you are trying to communicate with your long-lost aunt who lives 2,000 miles away, you could actually *send* her a hug or handhold.

Though a strange idea, it might help people 'feel' their interaction over the internet better. And that will make them feel that their friend isn't so far away after all.

4. Xenotransplants

Have you ever thought about whether you'd like an animal body part on or in your body? It's fun to ask people this; you get all kinds of strange answers. Commonly, people will reply that they want wings to fly, or perhaps a tail to..., have a tail. The discussion is silly and fun but is becoming something that isn't totally out of the realm of possibility.

A Xenotransplant is transplanting the organs of an animal into a human, to try to keep them alive. Sometimes, people become very ill and require what is called a 'transplant.' This means that they need a new organ, or a bit of an organ, to keep them alive.

Unfortunately, it's difficult to find human organs, hospitals need more than they have access to, so scientists are trying desperately to find alternative options.

So far, there have been two examples of Xenotransplants that have involved using pig hearts. Pigs share a lot of similarities with humans and their organs can be used, with some tweaking, in humans.

The procedure is very early in development but is being explored as a real possibility in medical science. Would you want to accept an animal organ if it meant keeping you alive? Discuss this one with parents and friends. Is it a step too far?

5. 3D printing

This is cheating a bit, as 3D printing has been around for a short while now, so isn't technically just a future invention. People use 3D printers to create all sorts of things, and their ingenuity shows no signs of stopping. Sculptures, toys, weapons, and false limbs have all been created for a cheap price using 3D printers, and the technology could become increasingly important.

If you're unsure, 3D printers do what they say. They print things in 3D, so rather than text or an image on paper, a 3D printer creates a physical object instead. It's very intelligent and has caught the attention of medical professionals as a way to help mend our ailing bodies.

Ossiform, a 3D printing company, specializes in printing alternatives for human bones. They make the bones from special materials that make them safe to use inside the body and help change people's lives forever. If the business takes off, just imagine the possibilities!

As 3D printing is cheap compared to other ways of making things, so it could be affordable to most people. The printing could literally help people walk again after losing the ability in an accident. Or it could provide people with another finger (in case they misplace one). The technology is promising and could help us care for millions of people, for a tiny fee.

6. Giving back to Mother Earth

It's not nice to think about, but one day, all of us shall come to an end and we shall cease to be.

When this happens, usually one of two things happens:

1) Cremation, where the body is burned to ash, or
2) Burial, where the body is laid to rest in the earth.

Though these are traditional, they're not great for the environment. In fact, a cremation releases 882 lbs. of carbon dioxide into the atmosphere! That's as much as if you take a three-hour long plane ride. So, some companies are looking at other ways to say goodbye to our dearly departed and offer them a green and respectful way to bow out.

In some areas such as Washington, US, you can be composted, like people do with their food waste. They lay the body in a chamber with bark and soil, and over 30 days, your body is reduced to the soil. Your mulch is then scattered in woodlands or gardens.

A more 'futuristic' method is to use a 'mushroom suit.' The idea is that you're buried covered in tiny mushrooms and fungi, which then aid natural decomposition. This means that the body decays faster, and the harmful bacteria released when that happens are eaten up by the mushrooms. Neat!

The hurdle with 'new' funeral practices isn't usually the technology. It's what we call 'social acceptance.' This means that at the moment, most people would find these methods weird and don't like them, so maybe they won't become popular.

What do you think? Would you like to be composted or turned into mushroom gunk?

7. Robots

Let's not beat around the bush here! Robots are futuristic, they're in lots of movies, and they're cool. When are we going to have robots in our homes?

Unfortunately, the answer to that is 'maybe never.'

That isn't to say that robots aren't being made, not at all. Companies such as Boston Dynamics (YouTube - them!) are creating human-like robots that are beginning to function in an impressive way. Their robots can run, jump, balance, and hold things. This is a huge leap forward, and robots aren't that far off from being useful to humans. There's just one snag.

What about the 'brain' of the robot? The AI. As you read this book, there are debates occurring around the world as to whether or not we should allow robots to have AI. It might sound like a nightmare scenario that doesn't exist, but what if we make the robot so clever that it turns on us, humans? What if this leads to a war with robots? This is the sort of debate being had today, and no answer has yet been found.

So, maybe we're a bit far off C-3PO from *Star Wars*, but perhaps not. The world of robotics is very exciting and worth keeping an eye on. Would you like to have robots cleaning up your house? Or walking to the shops with you for company?

8. Self-driving cars

If you've ever been on a long car journey, then you'll know how *boring* they can be. Sure, you may be traveling hundreds of miles to visit somewhere outstanding, to relax, or to spend time with your family, but the journey in a car can be unbelievably dull.

As well as the whole 'dullness' of it all, human beings are prone to accidents. We crash cars sometimes. Cars are very dangerous; injuries and deaths occur every year across the world because of poor driving.

This is why companies across the world are developing cars that don't require anyone to drive them. You simply program in your destination, and off it goes.

The idea is that if you remove people from the whole 'car' thing, then it can be seamless. You won't have to have traffic lights because the cars will communicate using their technology, so they'll be able to avoid each other by mere centimeters. No traffic jams will happen because the cars won't crash. All in all, it should be a fantastic network of self-driving cars that do the job perfectly.

It's not quite there yet, however. Tesla and Mercedes-Benz are both working on different systems and have run into problems. The system might malfunction, and it crashes, or the car might fail to drive correctly, requiring a human to step in. Basically, it's not there yet, but it may not be far away!

Would you feel safe in a self-driving car? Why? Why not? Ask the drivers in your life and see what they think about it.

9. Virtual reality

Since the invention of video games, nerds across the world have dreamed of the day that they'd be able to put on a helmet and be *in* the game. That is, beamed in, ready to live their dreams as a pro sports player or a lone killing machine on the battlefield.

For decades, that idea seemed like a sci-fi fantasy that couldn't truly happen, but the last few years have shown that we're closer to it than ever before. Gaming geniuses and scientists have been working on making Virtual Reality headsets that allow gamers to feel like they're truly living the gaming experience. It's already impressive and has been added to the Christmas lists of children everywhere.

But where is it going next? VR is encompassing, but it's still a bit clunky. Some companies are investigating the idea of removing a handset altogether, meaning that you'd control what's happening without having to hold anything. Others have invented a 360-degree treadmill that allows you to actually run, making your character run too. Imagine going to a friend's house to play *Fortnite 3D* and being able to actually run, jump, and dive through the rounds, experiencing every thrill as if you were there.

It won't just be games either. Experts think that it won't be long before VR is being used in schools and universities, meaning that learning can be accomplished without having to go anywhere. Virtual holidays could be taken, instead of boarding a plane, and movies could be made that you experience in frightening detail.

What do you think is the limit for Virtual Reality? What would you like to use VR in the future?

10. Microchip payment

You might have noticed that how we pay for things has changed dramatically in the 21st century. It wasn't unusual for the average person to carry cash with them to pay in the early 2000s, but by the time 2010 rolled around, most people would use cards. Soon after, cards could use 'contactless' technology, meaning that small payments were carried out with a simple tap. Then mobile phones could do the same thing and we're now at a point where many countries hardly use cash at all, and some shops won't even accept it. The question is what's next for how we pay for things?

Well, some people are ahead of the game on this one. If you go to a company called Walletmor, they'll implant a microchip into your hand for a small price of €250. That microchip will enable you to pay, via contactless payment, at any card machine that takes it.

Some experts think that this is just the beginning of the whole 'chip in the hand' thing. In the next 20–30 years, microchips could carry more and more information about us, and it may even become compulsory to have them. Microchips could carry data on your name, address, job, and financial information. Microchips could even replace the passport in time.

What do you think about this? Talk to your friends and family about the fact that microchips in the hand are possible now. Would they get it?

That was just a small glimpse into our futuristic world. Some of these ideas are frightening to many people, and it's normal to feel like that. Keep up to date on technological innovations and make sure you talk to people about them. Remember as well that many of these proposed changes will be different from what they are now, and they're being studied for the betterment of humankind.

Who knows how life will look in 2040?

WHAT MAKES
A MYTHICAL CREATURE?

Across the centuries and millennia, humankind has constructed mythical creatures that have baffled, entertained, and confused.

A mythical creature is one that doesn't exist but is a part of our culture. These creatures might have magical powers or possess some capabilities beyond us mere humans. What we're going to consider in this chapter is, where these creatures came from. When was the first fairy thought of? And what about trolls?

As well as looking at genuine mythological beings, you'll hear about the stories behind some unfortunate animals that were assumed *not* to be real. The poor creatures who were assumed to not exist!

This chapter is about questioning what we know to be true. If people didn't believe that platypuses were real, then can we definitely know that fairies aren't real? Probably, yes, but ask yourself, "What makes a mythical creature?" and think about that as you read these deep, intriguing, bizarre, and sometimes just silly stories.

1. Narwhals

If you haven't seen a narwhal before, then you'd find the creature a bit strange. Narwhals are ocean-dwelling animals that have a body a bit like a sea lion. The major difference is that the narwhal has a large horn on its head. That's what earned it the nickname 'the unicorn of the sea.' Narwhals were also used as inspiration for the monster in Jules Verne's classic novel *Eighty Thousand Leagues Under the Sea.*

The horn isn't actually a horn, but a tusk, and it was sold during the Middle Ages as a unicorn horn to gullible customers. Poor medieval peasants thought it had magical properties and could cure forms of sickness or misfortune. In reality, it's just a long, thin tusk that protrudes from the friendly-looking narwhal.

All this talk of narwhals and unicorns, however, has led many people to struggle to be sure if narwhals are real or not. The narwhal has been made into a legend throughout human history and to this day, 15,000 people google the question "Are narwhals real?" every month.

Narwhals are very much real and aren't dangerous leviathans or magical creatures. But many people perhaps wish that they were.

2. Platypuses

The duck-billed platypus is a strange-looking animal, no one can deny that. They are mammals and have the body of a beaver, with a duck-like bill, and they lay eggs (which mammals don't do). Platypuses are native to Australia and when English zoologist George Shaw found one in 1799, he felt that he had to bring it back to England.

However, Shaw wasn't presenting the platypus as an example of natural wonder from the other side of the world. No. Instead, Shaw was making the case that the platypus was obviously a hoax by some mad scientist!

He felt that someone could easily have taken a beaver's body and a duck's bill and simply stitched them together for some strange prank. He even cut the skin of the platypus he'd found to find the stitches, which he wasn't able to do. Scientists across England and Europe were baffled by the small animal, and all were convinced that it wasn't real.

You might think they sound foolish, but in 1799, the platypus was a lot to wrap your head around. In Europe, no mammal had been discovered with reptile features (like laying eggs), so that was assumed to be impossible. It took a few years for scientists and zoologists to be convinced that it was a real animal. Though, of course, Indigenous Australians had known about platypuses for thousands of years and didn't need any convincing of it!

3. Trolls

Trolls feature in countless forms of popular culture all over the world. *Harry Potter, Lord of the Rings, Dungeons & Dragons,* and numerous video games present them as slow, dim-witted enemies of the "good guys." Trolls are typically shown to be large, human-like creatures, possessing a great deal of strength and a great lack of brain. But where did they come from? And why have they been used so much in our media?

Trolls originated in Scandinavian folklore. Scandinavia is the area comprising countries such as Norway, Denmark, and Sweden. Early in Scandinavian mythology, trolls were family groups that lived in the mountains. They didn't like humans particularly and tried to stay away from them. Over time this changed, and trolls grew to possess the more grotesque visuals we know today.

Scandinavian folklore states that trolls turn to stone in the sunlight, and many natural landmarks are said to be trolls that were caught out. Large rock faces, cliffs, and mountains are attributed to mythological tales of a troll who didn't get back to their home in time.

Stories of trolls have been told for hundreds of years to frighten children or as a warning not to stay out too late after dark. The stories went from being only Scandinavian to being spoken about all over Europe, which has helped them become key figures in so much fantastical popular culture.

4. Fairies

Fairies are another mythological creature that has stood the test of time. Children's books are still written about fairies, and they're represented in classic stories such as *Cinderella*, *Pinocchio*, *Peter Pan*, and *A Midsummer Night's Dream*. They're everywhere. Now that the word 'fairy' has been written, you've probably been thinking of a tiny, glowing person with wings.

It's also important to note that some people do believe that fairies exist and aren't just animals of legend. Societies worked in the early 1900s to prove their existence, with a series of famous photos of the so-called *Cottingley Fairies* being used as evidence. This was later proved to be photo manipulation.

Real or not, they're a constant of human culture. They represent something magical and normally have special powers that humans don't. In most instances, fairies are kind to people and try to make their lives better, which may be why companies such as Disney like using them in their films so much.

Fairies come from many locations across Europe. They emerged sometime in the 1st millennium CE when instances of good fortune were attributed to fairies. If your farm had a good harvest, it might have been magical fairies. If you found something that had been lost for months, it was the fairies that found it for you.

Some cultures, however, show fairies to be evil beings, who use their powers for malice and bad actions. In some parts of England, people would carry good luck charms, such as a four-leaf clover, to ward off fairies, or they'd start wearing their clothing inside out.

Nice or nasty, fairies have been around for thousands of years, remaining a powerful image in most cultures across the world.

5. Gorillas

If you were told of a vicious, human-like creature with dark fur that possessed strength ten times that of a man, what would you think? Nowadays, you might correctly guess what the animal is, but for hundreds of years, the gorilla wasn't known about.

Since the 5th century BCE, explorers had told tales and listened to reports of vicious, supernatural, human devils that tore into campsites and destroyed them. For a long time, scientists and explorers were undecided about what the creature was. Some assumed that it had been made up or had died out.

It wasn't until 1847 that they realized it was the gorilla, due to scientists discovering the animal. That seems remarkably late to 'discover' a gorilla, but Western scientists simply hadn't had the chance to meet one any earlier! The explorer Paul Du Chaillu was the first westerner to see a live gorilla during his travel through western equatorial Africa from 1856 to 1859.

Perhaps many of the stories of the yeti or the bigfoot descend from the misunderstood gorilla, but for a long time, people assumed that there was no way a creature of such viciousness could even exist.

And this was years before *King Kong* was released!

6. Dragons

Dragons have had a remarkably big impact on the world, considering that they don't exist. Different cultures have different dragons, but generally, they're large lizard-type things that have some form of magical ability. In Ancient China, the dragons were long and thin, looking almost like a snake. Whereas, in Europe, dragons were shown to be fire-breathing, with huge wings.

The Image of the dragon has lived on for centuries, and the mythological monster continues to amaze us today. Dragons feature in fantasy franchises like *Harry Potter, Game of Thrones, Elder Scrolls*, and *The Lord of the Rings*. They also still hold a place in literature, appearing in books such as *Eragon, Discworld,* and *How to Train Your Dragon.*

The question is: Where did they come from?

The origins of dragons can be traced back to ancient times, when they were referenced in Ancient Greece and Ancient Egypt. Dragons were often depicted as holding a great deal of wisdom, and as guardians of treasures or protectors of secrets that were to be overcome by heroes. As time passed by, the image of dragons spread farther into Eastern Asia and changed during the Medieval period.

In Medieval England, the story of St. George slaying an evil dragon became popular, and dragons were seen as monstrous beings that were to be slain. Stories of slaying dragons told of ridding lands of evil but were really about Christianity and the power of God.

Dragons have served as symbols of evil, wisdom, strength, and protection, and they remain very significant to many different cultures. They continue to capture our imaginations in books, films, and video games and will likely do so for many more decades to come.

7. Giant squids

If you've seen the *Pirates of the Caribbean*, then you may have seen the legendary Kraken taking on Captain Jack Sparrow. The Kraken is a gargantuan, grotesque squid that can gobble up a ship, along with its crew, in a matter of seconds.

The Kraken emerged from Nordic legend but was generally assumed not to be real. Tales of an enormous monster living in the darkest reaches of the ocean seemed far-fetched, even to sailors a thousand years ago.

But what if the assumptions were wrong? In the 1850s, a Norwegian scientist became obsessed with finding the Kraken. He ended up writing papers on the existence of the animal and ships began to find huge parts of squids in the ocean.

Theories emerged about the existence of the giant squid, and in the 20th century, they were finally confirmed, without doubt, to exist in 2004. A team of scientists in Japan launched a deep-sea expedition and were the first to video a live giant squid, in its natural habitat - and it was indeed giant.

Giant squids grow, we think, to be at least 33 feet long. Not quite the size of the Kraken, but big enough for sure! They remain elusive, and work is constantly being carried out to find out more. They live so far down in the ocean that it's difficult to even reach them, let alone carry out complicated experiments. Perhaps there's an even larger squid waiting in an undiscovered part of our planet's seas, lurking in the darkness...

8. Rhinoceroses / unicorns

In the 1st century CE, a man called Pliny the Elder wrote about the unicorn. Pliny was a Roman naturalist and was exceptionally clever. He found the amazing animal and documented it as best as he could. Here's what he had to say:

"It has the head of a stag, the feet of an elephant, and the tail of a boar. It makes a deep sound and has a single black horn which projects from the middle of its forehead."

Not quite the rainbow-projecting, graceful horse that comes to mind when we think 'unicorn' then. No, instead, it's likely, the ancient tales of unicorns that came from the time of Pliny were just descriptions of…, a rhinoceros.

Over the years, the image of the unicorn changed and became the sleek, beautiful picture that we have today. The unicorn (the horse one) is now the national animal of Scotland and is a staple in children's books and TV shows, but it's funny to think that it all started because someone didn't know how to say "rhinoceros."

9. Leprechauns

The leprechaun has been an image associated with Ireland for centuries. Leprechauns are mischievous and elusive, shown to be small men dressed in green aprons and pointed hats. Every year, on St. Patrick's Day, people dress up as leprechauns. The creature is said to leave gold at the end of rainbows. But where did this all come from?

The leprechaun comes from Ancient Irish beliefs, and they were part of a larger folk story. Unlike other beings, leprechauns are seen as tricksters and out for themselves rather than seeking to help anyone. According to legend, leprechauns live in the Irish countryside, in burrows and trees. They can appear and disappear in an instant and horde untold treasures in secret locations.

The legend of the leprechaun has grown over time, and they've been highlighted in many forms of media. Lucky Charms remains one of the most loved cereals in America and features a leprechaun as the face of the brand. The Boston Celtics' mascot is a leprechaun called Lucky, and an entire movie franchise called *Leprechaun* achieved worldwide success beginning in 1993.

The leprechaun is a mythological creature that is here to stay. Next time you see a rainbow, try to think of a tiny man, dressed in green, stashing his gold at the end of it and giggling because you'll never find it.

10. Okapis

Okapis might take the title for being the most elusive animal of all time. You probably don't even know what it looks like, so a quick google may be in order.

An okapi is a four-legged herbivore that looks a bit like a cross between a zebra and a giraffe. It has black-and-white striped legs, a sleek brown coat, and pricked-up ears. It's an unusual creature.

It's so unusual, in fact, that until 1902, it was thought to be a myth. Despite claims from people living in Africa and explorers, they had never been proven to exist, which led to the creature being called the 'African Unicorn,' but they do not have a unicorn horn. Scientists were convinced that no such animal could exist; if it had, then surely it would have been documented properly at some stage.

Okapis can be found in some zoos, but that doesn't mean there are many of them around. In fact, it wasn't even seen on camera in the wild until 2008 when a motion-triggered camera caught one in the jungles of the Democratic Republic of Congo.

We doubted okapis for centuries because it just seemed so bizarre to scientists, and the fact that it remained so hidden until the 21st century is remarkable.

So closes our examination of mythical creatures and misunderstood mythical creatures. It's amazing to see that many made-up animals continue to be important to us human beings. Our television, movies, and books regularly draw on our common awareness of all things mythical and magical to craft worlds for us to enjoy. There are many more examples to investigate across the world of all things made up, and you'll only be more intrigued by what you discover.

It's even more fun to question what we *think* isn't real, like what was formerly thought of okapis or platypuses but could be hiding somewhere in our fantastical world. Every single week, new animals are discovered in the Mariana Trench in the Pacific

Ocean or the rainforests of South America. Who knows what secrets are set to be revealed to us?

10 THINGS YOU DIDN'T KNOW ABOUT YOUR ANUS

In this chapter, we discuss your anus.

Your anus is the circular hole in your backside, out of which poop comes out. It's important that you take this very seriously, and try to learn as much as you can. So, this won't be a funny chapter at all.

Only kidding, this is really very silly - but it can also be great fun to learn as much as we can about our very, very secret area. Humans want to know so little about that area, but it's actually very important to investigate. The butthole is one of the most important parts of you. It lets you dispose of waste effectively, and if you couldn't do that, then you would literally die.

Enjoy reading ten facts you probably didn't know about your own bum, and make sure you bring them up at dinner, so everyone tells you off for being utterly disgusting.

1. What is the anus?

We're going to use a few words throughout this chapter about "where the sun don't shine," so let's define some so you know what we're talking about.

Your anus is the opening in the human body between the buttocks. It's at the end of your digestive system, and it's where poop comes out. Got it? Good!

Your digestive system is a series of organs and squishy bits in the middle of your body that help extract all the good stuff from food. The system then turns into poop in the colon and passes it onto the rectum, where it waits before being expelled through the anus.

The process is really important and helps extract the energy that you need to get you through every day. We don't like to talk about it much, but we should! It's frankly amazing.

If you get confused at any point, refer back to these definitions to remind yourself what we're talking about!

2. There's more than one way to a clean bum

You might think that wiping one's bottom is a simple task, with one answer to it. You put some toilet paper in the correct zone until it starts to come back clean. Well, it hasn't always been that way.

In fact, toilet paper wasn't invented until 1857, which leaves thousands and thousands of years without it. People weren't just walking around having not properly cleaned up their mess, however; that would lead to serious problems, the least of which would be the smell. So, what were people doing?

For a time, people would just use whatever they could get hold of to wipe their back passage. Be that sticks, leaves, or stones. That might sound a little uncomfortable, but you just make sure that you don't put the stick in the wrong way up.

More sophisticated methods were used such as water and a cloth to properly clean up afterward. Many cultures continue to employ water in the bathroom for the same reason. You can't clean a car with just a sponge. You need a hose too, so why not do the same for your bum?

Animal furs were used by the Medieval period, as were shellfish and corn on the cob. But most of the time, people simply used their hands.

Never thought you'd be grateful for single-ply toilet paper, did you? Next time you want to complain it's too thin, imagine having to use a stone.

3. Two sphincters

You may have heard of the 'sphincter' before; it's often used as a term for your butthole. However, a sphincter is a word that just means a 'ring of muscle,' which is exactly what your anus is. The thing is - you don't just have one of them.

No, your anus actually has *two*. One of them is more internal, while one is external. You have control of your external sphincter. If you've ever desperately needed the bathroom before but find yourself irritatingly far away, you'll notice that you have this control. After a certain age, you're able to control it very well so that you don't simply poop when out with your friends.

However, you have no control over your internal sphincter. This one does as it's supposed to, and you can't override it. When this one engages, you'll feel the need to visit the lavatory sharpish because it means that the next payload is on the way.

Thanks to that external sphincter! Without it, we'd all have ruined a few extra pairs of trousers.

4. 'Til gas do us fart

Awful title aside, we're going to talk about the expulsion of gas known as a 'fart.' Other nicknames include - guff, bottom-burp, crop-dusting, and gas-bomb.

When you're in the company of someone who's unleashed an expulsion of gas, it can be rather unpleasant. The gas smells awful, and it's just generally not fun to be nearby. But we don't like to admit that it's perfectly normal to perform a bum-trump.

In fact, the average person farts somewhere between 13 and 21 times per day!

Farting is an important process; it helps you get rid of gases from your body that build up during digestion. If you didn't ever pass gas, then the gas would build up with no hope of escape, and you could suffer a severe case of 'exploding bum syndrome.'

This isn't your excuse to start farting every few minutes, but perhaps it's your chance to be a bit kinder to someone when they do.

It's also worth pointing out that your farts are actually *flammable*. Farts contain methane, a highly flammable gas, and it can be set alight for a tiny flame effect. For safety reasons, do *not* try to do this - and definitely don't do it when behind a cow.

5. Stupid evolution stopping us all from having tails!

Have you ever fallen on your backside and felt a really sharp pain just above your bottom? It often feels like a stingy, bruise pain, and doing so can make sitting down painful for a few days.

When you do this, you're falling on a bone called the coccyx ("cock-six" is the pronunciation). The coccyx isn't protected by much fat or muscle, so falling on it can produce a very sharp pain, and you can even break it!

Thousands and thousands of years ago, the coccyx had an important use. It helped to give us humans structure and control over our tails. Over a long period, however, we lost our tails and now just have a bit of bone that exists only to cause pain.

Kind of upsetting to know we *once* had tails but now don't. Imagine all of the extra things you could do with a tail…, okay, not many, but we might have better balance.

6. Limit your visits to five minutes

Some people like to treat their toilet visits as an occasion. Either it's a chance to sit and idly scroll on their phones, or complete a bit more of the book they've been reading for the last year. It's becoming increasingly easy to spend ten or 15 minutes atop the porcelain throne in the 21st century.

However, this practice is strongly discouraged by doctors as it can cause health problems for your bottom. As you sit there, gravity exerts pressure on your backside and brings extra blood to the area. This can lead to things swelling up and maybe the development of hemorrhoids. Hemorrhoids are harmless, painful lumps that can occur in someone's bum and should be avoided.

So, if you want to avoid having a stinging circle of hell, get in there, do your business, and get out!

7. "Everything comes down to poo!"

There was once a famous and successful comedy show called *Scrubs*, focusing on the lives of young doctors and the difficulties of their jobs. In one memorable episode, two of the characters sing a jaunty song about how, when it comes to your health, "Everything comes down to poo!"

While that may not be all there is to it, your poop can be incredibly important if you find yourself unwell.

Your disposable nuggets contain a ton of information and DNA. Hospitals ask for a sample if there's a suspected problem within an aspect of your digestive system. By analyzing the brown gold, they can find out if you have deadly conditions such as cancer or if you have an infection or digestive issues.

All in all, your poop is pretty important and may one day save your life! Though don't start keeping samples around "just in case." If it's brown, flush it down.

8. There's hair there!

There comes a time in every person's life when they grow from a child into an adult. The process means a lot of change, and that can be difficult. Particularly when it comes to extra hair growth on your body.

This hair growth is completely natural and happens differently for different people, and this goes for your bottom too! Hair grows around your bum area, and it's totally normal, if a bit annoying.

Scientists aren't exactly sure why we continue to grow bum hair. There are many theories about why, such as that it helps produce our scent or prevents irritation in the region of Bum-donia; but no one knows why.

Just remember, if it's there, it's normal, so there's no need to panic unless it starts to look like you're wearing underpants even when you're not.

9. The powerhouse of the human

Your bottom is one of the most important parts of your body. It's almost constantly worked on as you walk around the place and is responsible for moving several crucial areas of the body.

Your main bottom muscle is the gluteus maximus, which is the largest muscle in the body. The GM helps to move your thighs and hips, all while keeping your torso upright and sturdy. That's a lot of work to do. If the GM wasn't so massive and strong, then humans wouldn't have evolved to walk in the way that we do.

If you work out your bottom muscles with exercises such as squats, lunges, and hip thrusts, then it can actually help to relieve back pain as you get older, which is definitely worth preventing.

Remember, a stronger bum means a better back, better posture, and tighter jeans.

10. Bum-powered propulsion

Lastly, this isn't really about *your* anus, unless you're a 992-pound, underwater colossus.

We're talking about the manatee, a large aquatic mammal found in the Caribbean and the waters surrounding America. The manatee is a funny-looking thing, covered in blubber and with a large, round nose. They can be quite friendly and, it transpires, quite speedy.

This is in part because manatees use their own jet propulsion to help them keep up speed in the water. Yep. Manatees fart to help control their speed and buoyancy in the ocean as they swim along. It's quite ingenious, using waste gas for a useful purpose, but you wouldn't want to be swimming in its wake!

That was a brief look into your anus, an examination of all things sphincterical and bumtacular! While a bit of a gross topic and taboo in social circles, it's important to know as much as possible about your body. In your life, someone (hopefully a doctor) will likely have to examine your rear end, and it just might save your life. The more you know about that area, the quicker you can tell if something is wrong. While it's important that you're aware of the features of your own cheeky landscape, you don't need to compare with anyone else!

10 THINGS YOU DIDN'T KNOW ABOUT URANUS

Now that we've finished detailing some of the interesting, though gross, facts about *your anus*, we'll now turn our attention to facts about *Uranus*.

Uranus can be pronounced like "your anus," but NASA prefers it if you say it like "yur-ah-noos," probably to stop people from making jokes about it.

Uranus is the seventh planet in the solar system, and our hopes of visiting it are very slim, but we do know a great deal about it already. Enjoy reading some incredible facts about one of the biggest, most inhospitable, and most mysterious planets that we know about.

1. Why is it called Uranus?

Uranus wasn't always a name that was snickered at by schoolchildren in a science class. The name has a heroic and God-related origin.

We named most of the planets in our solar system after Roman gods (Mercury, Venus, Mars, Jupiter, Saturn, Neptune, and ex-planet Pluto) - apart from Earth and Uranus. Uranus gets its name from the Greek god of the sky and the son of Chaos. Earth's name comes from a German word, meaning 'the ground'.

When the planet Uranus was discovered in 1781, there was a push for it to be named after George III, the King of England at the time. It was called George's Star (Georgium Sidus) by the British until 1850 when they conceded it was a stupid name and should be called Uranus instead.

2. A year on Uranus

Uranus is much further away from the Sun than we are, so it seems very unlikely that anything could ever live there. Because of its distance, it also experiences time differently to how we do on Earth. Here's what a 'year' would look and feel like on Uranus.

On average, the distance from the Sun to Uranus is 1.8 billion miles, which makes Earth's tiny 93 million miles look a bit pathetic. Because it's so far away, it takes the planet 84 Earth years to perform one rotation around the Sun.

The Uranus year experiences the seasons a bit like Earth does. Each half of the planet experiences winters that are 21 Earth years long and are almost completely dark.

At its coldest, Uranus reaches temperatures of -367.96 degrees Fahrenheit, and has wind speeds of almost 621 mph! NASA has observed clouds on the planet, but there's no oxygen, so there would be zero chance of humans being able to breathe on Uranus.

The most difficult job in the universe: working for Uranus' tourism board.

3. It's downright smelly!

Uranus smells of rotten eggs.

That's not just an insult, even less so an insult about your bottom. Rather, it's the absolute truth.

In 2018, incredibly clever scientists were able to determine what the upper layers of Uranus' atmosphere are made up of using a high-tech spectrograph. It turns out that the clouds in that layer consist of frozen hydrogen sulfide, which gives the flavor and stench of rotten eggs!

So, if anyone asks you if you know any space facts, confidently shout "Uranus smells of eggs!"

4. It could float if you had enough honey

Uranus is the second least-dense planet in the solar system. If something is dense, then it means that there's a lot of weight contained within not much space.

Most planets are very dense, but Uranus remains quite light compared to Earth - five times as light, in fact. The only planet that remains lighter is Saturn, which would be able to float in water, given the chance.

Uranus isn't quite as light, so unfortunately, it would fail to bob about in a vast ocean. However, if you had enough hard-working bees, then it *would* float in honey!

5. It has, selfishly, got 27 moons!

Twenty-seven moons! Here on Earth, we have only *one* moon, and we forget about it most of the time.

Most moons on other planets are named after more Roman and Greek mythological characters, but the moons of Uranus are unique. They are named after characters from works by William Shakespeare and Alexander Pope.

Moons become moons as they're either formed within the atmosphere of the planet or are pulled in by the planet's gravitational field. We think this has happened with Uranus, but scientists aren't yet sure about what many of the moons are even made of.

6. Uranus is showing

If you have perfect vision, then you might be lucky enough to actually *see* Uranus in the night sky.

Uranus exists at magnitude 5.3, which puts it just about within the brightness scale which means a human can see it. If you have eyesight that isn't perfect - so if you require glasses to see at your best - then you're very unlikely to catch it.

The thing is, even if you are blessed with perfect eyes, then you'll probably miss it anyway. You'd have to find yourself in an area with absolutely no light pollution and no clouds, somewhere that's miles from a city or town and human-made light. Even then, you'd need to know precisely where to look.

Many ancient astronomers saw Uranus in the sky but simply thought it was a bright star, which is why it wasn't recorded as a planet until the 1700s. If you use stargazing apps on a smartphone, you may stand a better chance of seeing it in the right conditions.

Good luck.

7. Humankind has visited it

Humans have made contact with Uranus but only once. Because of Uranus' hostile atmosphere and low temperatures, a metal spaceship will not survive for long. However, in 1986, NASA managed to get an unmanned craft close enough.

The craft was called the *Voyager 2*, and it got within 81,000 kilometers of the clouds of Uranus. Much closer and it would have been quickly destroyed. The *Voyager 2* took thousands and thousands of photographs of the planet and zoomed off toward Neptune, its nearest target.

Voyager 2 remains the only spacecraft to have studied all four of the solar system's giant planets at 'close range.' It was an amazing feat of space science. Several projects are being discussed all over the world, but currently, no plans have been confirmed regarding a re-visit to the inhospitable planet. Hopefully one day we'll see a human being brave enough to examine Uranus' surface.

8. Uranus is gigantic

Uranus is big. Really big. You'll say, "Well, obviously, it's a planet!" but *seriously*.

Uranus is one of the Giant Planets in our solar system, along with Jupiter, Saturn and Neptune. The Giant Planets are called such because they are..., well, they're giant.

Uranus could fit 63 Earths inside of it and has a diameter of over 15,534 miles. It's taken human beings thousands of years to explore our own planet; imagine how long it would take us to document the intricate areas of Uranus if we lived there!

Uranus and Neptune remain the only Ice Giant planets. They're so-called because the other two giants, Jupiter and Saturn, are Gas Giants and made from materials such as hydrogen and helium. Uranus and Neptune are made from heavier elements such as oxygen, water, methane, and ammonia. Their atmosphere consists of ice, which is yet another factor that makes them impossible for us to visit right now.

9. Uranus is the first planet to have been discovered using a telescope

It sounds almost impossible, but Uranus was the first planet ever discovered by using a telescope.

If you tell an amateur astronomer or stargazer not to use a telescope, they'll scoff and say you'll never see anything without it. This isn't technically true. As mentioned earlier, Uranus was discovered in the 1700s. In fact, it was 1781, to be precise. Astronomer William Herschel 'discovered' Uranus while searching for faint stars. In doing so, he found the first planet since the days of Ancient Rome.

The reason for this is that the Romans could see the planets at various times throughout the year. They'd charted them, named them, and had thus discovered Mercury, Venus, Mars, Saturn, and Jupiter. This left Uranus and Neptune waiting for the invention of the telescope.

You can see planets with the naked eye in good conditions at night, and it's worth looking at earthsky.org to find out what will be visible from where. Using your eyes, the planets will look like bright stars, but if you're lucky enough to procure a telescope, you may see a heck of a lot more.

10. Uranus is lopsided

In the solar system, most planets spin on a vertical axis, which gives them even and predictable seasons and weather conditions throughout the year. The problem is that Uranus doesn't do this; it spins on its side.

This is why Uranus experiences 21-year-long winters. The planet simply doesn't spin in the way it should. There's been speculation by scientists and astronauts that Uranus was hit hundreds of thousands of years ago by a huge object. The object would have to be about the size of our planet to do serious damage, and the collision must have been so strong that the planet was knocked off of its axis.

Uranus, therefore, settled at a 97-degree tilt and now experiences the most extreme seasons in the entire solar system. Venus also spins in this same way, which could be due to the same reason. But given the closer proximity of Venus to the Sun, it's not impacted in the same way as Uranus.

So, there you have it! Ten facts about Uranus. Next time you're in a science lesson, or with friends who laugh at the planet, you can bring up a litany of interesting and surprising facts about the giant. You'll look extremely clever, and everyone will think that you're unable to take a joke, but it'll be worth it.

CONCLUSION

Here we are then, at the end of our mammoth journey through a universe of facts, tidbits, stories, and hairy bums. Hopefully, you've enjoyed reading through it. It doesn't matter if you skimmed parts of it, not particularly interested in what it had to say. Nor does it matter if you combed through each sentence with a fine toothcomb, desperate to find the tasty morsels of information. All that really matters is that you enjoyed it.

Each chapter had ten main 'facts' in it, but what you'll have noticed (if you are really, *really* clever) is that you didn't just get ten facts per chapter. There are an estimated 4,072 facts in this book, and that's just guesswork by some properly clever people. This book has been carefully designed to burst with knowledge and to be fun to read, unlike so many boring things we have to do in our lives.

It's unlikely that at school, college, or university, you'll end up enrolling in a class called "Bumology and Anus Facts" or "The Art of Fart." But hopefully, hidden within this maze of interest, there are areas in which you are genuinely interested.

Think about the topics that this book covers. There are loads:

History, Space, Physics, Biology, Zoology, Cryptozoology, Social Studies, Cultural Studies, Geography, English Literature,

Psychology, Criminology, and Bum Studies. The only thing missing is Math because, let's be honest, it's not very fun.

If you read about a topic within this book that tickled your fancy, then you are encouraged to investigate it further. The best thing to do, as always, is to ask someone who's older or more experienced in life to help you do so. Some topics can become really complicated, scary, or just unpleasant when you investigate them further, so please make sure you're responsible if you want to further your education.

If there's a lesson to learn from this book then it's this: Learning can be fantastic fun and really silly. Learning isn't just completed in classrooms, it's in every part of our lives. We spend decades and decades learning and accumulating knowledge. Elderly people know so much because they've spent *so long* learning and experiencing things for themselves! It's good to celebrate knowing things, and it's good to celebrate the chance to deliberately make yourself more knowledgeable.

If you don't know where to start, then get yourself another fact or general knowledge book and read that one too. To be fair, probably don't get another one that's called *Ten Things You Didn't Know About Uranus*, because it'll cover a lot of what you've just read about.

Use this book to make quizzes, to entertain, and to help you be a super clever big brain as you live your life. The book will always be there waiting for you, eager to be read again. So, if you forget what you have read, or figure that it might just be worth another skimming, then come right on back.

Thank you for reading *Ten Things You Didn't Know About Uranus.* Have fun learning, have fun living, and have fun telling people that they've got hairy bums that smell like Uranus!

Made in the USA
Las Vegas, NV
12 December 2023

82715949R00085